THE
MERCHANT
OF VENICE

HARCOURT SHAKESPEARE

THE
MERCHANT
OF VENICE
SECOND EDITION

Series Editor: Ken Roy

edited by
Ian Waldron and Mark Maitman

Harcourt Canada

Orlando Austin New York San Diego Toronto London

National Library of Canada Cataloguing in Publication

Shakespeare, William, 1564–1616
          The merchant of Venice / edited by Mark Maitman and Ian Waldron—2nd ed.

(Harcourt Shakespeare)
For use in high schools.
ISBN 0-7747-1482-4

          I. Maitman, Mark II. Waldron, Ian III. Title. IV. Series.

PR2825.A2M342 2003   822.3'3   C2003-904247-2

Harcourt Shakespeare: Series Editor, Ken Roy

Project Manager: Terry-Lee Wheelband
Developmental Editor: J.J. Wilson
Production Editor: Tricia Carmichael
Production Coordinators: Kimberly Sullivan, David Ward
Page Composition: Rachel Rosen
Cover and Text Illustrations: Marika and Laszlo Gal

∞ Printed in Canada on acid-free paper.
1 2 3 4 5   07 06 05 04 03

To the Reader

This edition of *The Merchant of Venice* has been designed to encourage your active participation in the dramatic experience of Shakespeare's play.

Before reading each scene in the play, you will have an opportunity to explore ideas, themes, or personal experiences similar to the ones you will read about. You might want to discuss your opinions in small groups or, perhaps, record your responses in a journal.

As you begin to read each scene, a brief note will provide you with an outline of events within the scene, freeing you to think about the characters, their concerns and personalities, their relationships, and their interactions.

The notes of explanation that accompany Shakespeare's script are intended to speed your reading and enrich your enjoyment and understanding of the play. You will discover your own way of using them to your advantage. Be careful never to let them interfere with your experience of the play itself. You can always return to some of the longer historical notes after your first reading of each scene.

Each scene is followed by a set of activities related to the scene's themes and problems. You might want to explore these activities after each scene, after a group of scenes, or at the end of each act. Whichever you decide, you will discover that many of these activities, like the ones before each scene, call for group work and personal responses.

Your study of the play will be more efficient and productive if you maintain an organized approach. With your teacher, decide on what this approach will be. It might include a notebook for answers to general questions, a personal journal or reading log, a writing folder for creative explorations and compositions, or a director's log or script book.

Now that you have some idea about how the text will be presented in the pages that follow, you are ready to experience the play.

Getting Started

If this is your first Shakespearean play, take some time to discover how his plays would have been presented in his own time by searching the Internet using the entry "Shakespeare's Globe Theatre." You also might want to explore the medieval city of Venice on the Internet.

Although *The Merchant of Venice* is set in medieval times, the issues and concerns that Shakespeare presents in the play are surprisingly contemporary. You might want to take some time before you actually begin the text of the play to discuss some of the following questions in small groups and record in your journal some of your classmates' responses, particularly those you find interesting or thought-provoking. Another possibility is to record your own thoughts on these issues in a series of personal journal entries.

1. In our society, friendship is valued very highly. So is money. Which do you value more? What differences in personality and behaviour do you notice between those who value friends above all else and those who value money most?

2. "Don't judge a book by its cover!" What do you think this common saying means? What personal experiences have made you more aware that appearances can be deceptive? What happens to those who put their trust in appearances?

3. Should children obey their parents? Why or why not? Under what circumstances might a parent not deserve obedience from his or her children? When is a young person old enough to replace blind obedience with independent thought?

4. When many members of a society share a prejudice, they often discriminate against those who are in some way different. Have you ever been the victim of someone else's prejudice? What form did that prejudice take? How did you deal with it?

Return to these questions and your answers as you study the text. You will find that they provide you with a focus for discussing and writing about the play.

Dramatis Personae:
Literally, these Latin words mean "Masks of the Play." In Greek and Roman times, actors wore masks. Today, and in Shakespeare's day, the title simply means "Characters."

clown:
In the Elizabethan theatre, this term was not necessarily used to describe professional comedians, but, more commonly, it referred to an uneducated rustic, a "country bumpkin," a "hick."

waiting-maid:
She waits upon (serves) her mistress.

Magnificoes:
Venetian noblemen of great influence and wealth whose appearance, of course, would be truly "magnificent"

Gaoler:
early spelling (still used in Great Britain) for *jailer*

seat:
traditional family residence, estate

Continent:
the continent of Europe. As a set of islands, Venice itself was *not* considered part of the continent.

Dramatis Personae
(Characters in the Play)

Duke of Venice
Prince of Morocco ⎫
Prince of Arragon   ⎬ suitors to Portia
Antonio, the merchant of Venice
Bassanio, his friend
Solanio   ⎫
Salerio   ⎬ friends to Antonio and Bassanio
Gratiano ⎭
Lorenzo, in love with Jessica
Shylock, a Jew
Tubal, a Jew, his friend
Launcelot Gobbo, a clown, servant to Shylock, afterward to
  Bassanio
Old Gobbo, father to Launcelot
Leonardo, servant to Bassanio
Balthazar ⎫
Stephano   ⎬ servants to Portia
Portia, a rich heiress
Nerissa, her waiting-maid
Jessica, daughter to Shylock
**Magnificoes of Venice, Officers of the Court of Justice, Gaoler,
  Servants, and other Attendants**

Scene: Partly at Venice and partly at Belmont, the seat of Portia,
  on the Continent

Act 1, Scene 1

In this scene . . .

The play begins in Venice. Antonio, a merchant and nobleman, is in low spirits. His companions assume he is worried about his trading ships, but we learn that he is more concerned about Bassanio, his best friend. Bassanio is in debt, having wasted all of his own money and the money he has previously borrowed from Antonio. Furthermore, Bassanio now finds himself with a new concern. He has fallen in love with Portia, a wealthy and beautiful heiress. If he marries her, his financial problems will be solved. Without money, however, he cannot afford to travel to Belmont, where she lives, and become one of her many suitors.

Antonio has no money to give Bassanio, but he promises to use his reputation as an honest and reliable merchant to borrow the cash Bassanio needs to seek Portia's hand in marriage.

1	*In sooth:* in truth, truthfully; *sad:* serious, solemn, thoughtful (not simply unhappy)
5	*I am to learn:* I have yet to learn (I do not know)
6	*want-wit:* lack-wit, a person who lacks wit or intelligence
7	*ado:* to do (that is, difficulty or trouble)
9	*argosies:* large merchant ships; *portly:* billowing, swelling
10	*signiors:* gentlemen, noblemen; *burghers:* citizens; *flood:* sea
11	*pageants:* floats in a parade
12	*overpeer:* look down upon (What attitude is implied?); *petty traffickers:* small and insignificant trading boats
15	*had I:* if I had. This reversal of word order is very common in Shakespeare's plays. Watch for it again. *venture:* business "adventure," suggesting risk and uncertainty of gain or loss
16	*affections:* thoughts and feelings
18	*Plucking the grass:* to toss it into the air to see which way the wind is blowing
19	*roads:* anchorages (sheltered waters near the shore where ships may lie safely at anchor)
21	*out of doubt:* certainly
22	*wind:* breath; *broth:* soup
23	*ague:* fever
25-26	*I should not see . . . But . . . think:* if I saw . . . then I would think
26	*flats:* sandbars
27	*Andrew:* typical name for a merchant ship, used here by Salerio for the imaginary ship he creates; *dock'd:* run aground
28-29	*Vailing her high-top . . . her burial:* (What happened to the ship after it ran aground?)
29-31	*Should I go to church . . . and not bethink me:* if I were to go to church . . . would I not think?
30	*holy edifice:* altar
31	*straight:* straight away, immediately
32	*touching but:* simply by touching

Act 1, Scene 1

Venice. A street.

Enter Antonio, Salerio, and Solanio.

Antonio: In sooth, I know not why I am so sad:
It wearies me; you say it wearies you;
But how I caught it, found it, or came by it,
What stuff 'tis made of, whereof it is born,
I am to learn;   5
And such a want-wit sadness makes of me,
That I have much ado to know myself.
Salerio: Your mind is tossing on the ocean,
There, where your argosies with portly sail,
Like signiors and rich burghers on the flood,   10
Or, as it were, the pageants of the sea,
Do overpeer the petty traffickers,
That curtsy to them, do them reverence,
As they fly by them with their woven wings.
Solanio: Believe me, sir, had I such venture forth,   15
The better part of my affections would
Be with my hopes abroad. I should be still
Plucking the grass to know where sits the wind;
Peering in maps for ports, and piers, and roads;
And every object that might make me fear   20
Misfortune to my ventures, out of doubt
Would make me sad.
Salerio: My wind, cooling my broth,
Would blow me to an ague, when I thought
What harm a wind too great might do at sea.
I should not see the sandy hour-glass run   25
But I should think of shallows and of flats,
And see my wealthy Andrew dock'd in sand
Vailing her high-top lower than her ribs
To kiss her burial. Should I go to church
And see the holy edifice of stone,   30
And not bethink me straight of dangerous rocks,
Which touching but my gentle vessel's side

33-34   *spices . . . silks:* (Where would the *Andrew* have picked up this cargo, and where would she be taking it?)

35   *in a word:* briefly

35-36   *but even now . . . worth nothing:* (What physical gesture would Salerio use to illustrate his point in these lines?)

38   *bechanc'd:* if it happened

41   *fortune:* good luck

42   *one bottom:* the hold of a single ship

43-44   *nor is . . . present year:* I have not risked all my wealth on this year's voyages. Antonio uses "fortune" to suggest both luck (or chance) and wealth.

46   *Fie, fie!:* Nonsense! Don't be ridiculous!

50   *two-headed Janus:* a Roman god with two faces, one happy and one sad

51   *fram'd:* created

52   *evermore peep . . . eyes:* have eyes that are always narrowed from smiling

53   *parrots:* Parrots were considered to be stupid and foolish birds at the time.

54   *vinegar aspect:* sour disposition

56   *Nestor:* the oldest and wisest of the Greek chieftains who fought in the Trojan War. His name has come to suggest the wisdom of age and experience, but seldom laughter.

57   *kinsman:* Solanio means close friend rather than relative.

64   *embrace th' occasion:* take this opportunity

67   *You grow exceeding strange:* You have almost become a stranger (that is, we hardly ever see you anymore).

68   *We'll make . . . yours:* We'll arrange our free time to fit yours.

Would scatter all her spices on the stream,
Enrobe the roaring waters with my silks;
And, in a word, but even now worth this,   35
And now worth nothing? Shall I have the thought
To think on this, and shall I lack the thought
That such a thing bechanc'd would make me sad?
But tell not me: I know Antonio
Is sad to think upon his merchandise.   40
Antonio: Believe me, no: I thank my fortune for it,
    My ventures are not in one bottom trusted,
    Nor to one place; nor is my whole estate
    Upon the fortune of this present year:
    Therefore, my merchandise makes me not sad.   45
Solanio: Why, then you are in love.
Antonio: Fie, fie!
Salerio: Not in love neither? Then let us say you are sad
    Because you are not merry: and 'twere as easy
    For you to laugh and leap, and say you are merry
    Because you are not sad. Now, by two-headed Janus,   50
    Nature hath fram'd strange fellows in her time:
    Some that will evermore peep through their eyes,
    And laugh like parrots at a bag-piper;
    And other of such vinegar aspect
    That they'll not show their teeth in way of smile,   55
    Though Nestor swear the jest be laughable.
    [*Enter Bassanio, Lorenzo, and Gratiano*]
Solanio: Here comes Bassanio, your most noble kinsman,
    Gratiano, and Lorenzo. Fare ye well:
    We leave you now with better company.
Salerio: I would have stay'd till I had made you merry,   60
    If worthier friends had not prevented me.
Antonio: Your worth is very dear in my regard.
    I take it, your own business calls on you,
    And you embrace th' occasion to depart.
Salerio: Good morrow, my good lords.   65
Bassanio: Good signiors both, when shall we laugh? say,
        when?
    You grow exceeding strange: must it be so?
Salerio: We'll make our leisures to attend on yours.
                            [*Exeunt Salerio and Solanio*]

11

73-75	*You look . . . much care:* (How does Gratiano echo the comments of Salerio and Solanio?)
74	*You have too much respect:* You are worrying too much.
76	*marvellously:* greatly, much
77	*hold:* consider

82	*mortifying:* dying
84	*cut in alabaster:* sculpted in marble (probably on his tomb)
85	*jaundice:* a liver disease, in Elizabethan times associated with bad temper
86	*peevish:* bad-tempered
88	*visages:* faces
89	*Do cream and mantle:* develop a white surface scum
90-92	*And do . . . profound conceit:* and put on a show of being solemn in order to create an impression of being very intelligent
93	*As who:* as though he; *Oracle:* prophet. The ancient Greeks believed the gods spoke through the voice of an oracle known for great wisdom and foresight. The name Sir Oracle makes a mockery of this elevated position.
96-97	*only are reputed . . . nothing:* are considered to be wise only because they say nothing
97-99	*when, I am very sure . . . brothers fools:* If these quiet people *did* speak, everyone would realize that they were fools. The Bible threatens damnation to those who call their brothers fools (*Matthew* 5:22).
101-102	*But fish not . . . this opinion:* Do not fish for a reputation as a wise man by pretending to be serious (like the fools described in the previous lines). The gudgeon is a small European fish that is easily caught and often used as bait; metaphorically, it means a gullible person (one who will believe anything).
104	*exhortation:* earnest advice
106	*dumb:* silent, mute

Lorenzo: My Lord Bassanio, since you have found Antonio,
 We two will leave you; but, at dinner-time,   70
 I pray you, have in mind where we must meet.
Bassanio: I will not fail you.
Gratiano: You look not well, Signior Antonio;
 You have too much respect upon the world:
 They lose it that do buy it with much care.   75
 Believe me, you are marvellously chang'd.
Antonio: I hold the world but as the world, Gratiano;
 A stage where every man must play a part,
 And mine a sad one.
Gratiano: Let me play the fool:
 With mirth and laughter let old wrinkles come,   80
 And let my liver rather heat with wine
 Than my heart cool with mortifying groans.
 Why should a man, whose blood is warm within,
 Sit like his grandsire cut in alabaster,
 Sleep when he wakes, and creep into the jaundice   85
 By being peevish? I tell thee what, Antonio—
 I love thee, and 'tis my love that speaks—
 There are a sort of men whose visages
 Do cream and mantle like a standing pond,
 And do a wilful stillness entertain,   90
 With purpose to be dress'd in an opinion
 Of wisdom, gravity, profound conceit,
 As who should say, 'I am Sir Oracle,
 And when I ope my lips, let no dog bark!'
 O my Antonio, I do know of these   95
 That therefore only are reputed wise
 For saying nothing; when, I am very sure,
 If they should speak, would almost damn those ears
 Which, hearing them, would call their brothers fools.
 I'll tell thee more of this another time: 100
 But fish not, with this melancholy bait,
 For this fool-gudgeon, this opinion.
 Come, good Lorenzo. Fare ye well awhile:
 I'll end my exhortation after dinner.
Lorenzo: Well, we will leave you then till dinner-time.   105
 I must be one of these same dumb wise men,
 For Gratiano never lets me speak.

110   *I'll grow . . . this gear:* Your nonsensical argument has convinced me to talk more.

111   *i' faith:* in faith, in truth; *commendable:* praiseworthy

112   *neat's tongue dried:* smoked ox tongue; *maid not vendible:* unattractive young girl (with nothing to make her attractive other than the fact that she does not talk too much)

116   *chaff:* waste husks. The husks must be removed from wheat before it can be used to make flour.

117   *ere:* before

120   *pilgrimage:* a journey made to a holy place. The use of the word here implies that the lady in question is especially worthy of respect or reverence

124-125 *By something . . . continuance:* by living beyond my means

126-127 *Nor do I . . . noble rate:* And I do not complain about my loss of the rich life.

128   *to come fairly off from:* to repay fully and properly

129   *prodigal:* wasteful, extravagant

130   *gag'd:* engaged, bound, obligated

132   *warranty:* permission, agreement

133   *unburden:* reveal; *plots:* plans

138   *my extremest means:* "my last penny"

139   *occasions:* needs

140   *shaft:* arrow

141   *his fellow:* its companion (that is, another arrow)

142   *advised:* careful

143   *adventuring:* risking (Compare line 15 and lines 41–44.)

144   *oft:* often

145   *innocence:* childlike sincerity

Gratiano: Well, keep me company but two years more,
   Thou shalt not know the sound of thine own tongue.
Antonio: Fare you well: I'll grow a talker for this gear.   110
Gratiano: Thanks, i' faith; for silence is only commendable
   In a neat's tongue dried and a maid not vendible.
                              [*Exeunt Gratiano and Lorenzo*]
Antonio: Is that anything now?
Bassanio: Gratiano speaks an infinite deal of nothing, more
   than any man in all Venice. His reasons are as two   115
   grains of wheat hid in two bushels of chaff: you shall
   seek all day ere you find them, and when you have
   them, they are not worth the search.
Antonio: Well, tell me now, what lady is the same
   To whom you swore a secret pilgrimage,   120
   That you today promis'd to tell me of?
Bassanio: 'Tis not unknown to you, Antonio,
   How much I have disabled mine estate,
   By something showing a more swelling port
   Than my faint means would grant continuance: 125
   Nor do I now make moan to be abridg'd
   From such a noble rate; but my chief care
   Is, to come fairly off from the great debts
   Wherein my time, something too prodigal,
   Hath left me gag'd. To you, Antonio,   130
   I owe the most, in money and in love;
   And from your love I have a warranty
   To unburden all my plots and purposes
   How to get clear of all the debts I owe.
Antonio: I pray you, good Bassanio, let me know it;   135
   And if it stand, as you yourself still do,
   Within the eye of honour, be assur'd,
   My purse, my person, my extremest means,
   Lie all unlock'd to your occasions.
Bassanio: In my school-days, when I had lost one shaft,   140
   I shot his fellow of the self-same flight
   The self-same way with more advised watch,
   To find the other forth; and by adventuring both,
   I oft found both. I urge this childhood proof,
   Because what follows is pure innocence.   145
   I owe you much, and (like a wilful youth)

148   *self:* same

150-151 *or . . . Or:* either . . . or

151   *latter hazard:* second risk (that is, a second loan)

152   *rest:* remain

154   *circumstance:* "beating around the bush"

155   *out of doubt:* certainly

156   *In making question . . . uttermost:* by questioning my will-
        ingness to do all I can

160   *prest:* committed, ready

161   *lady richly left:* heiress

162   *fair:* beautiful. This is almost always Shakespeare's meaning,
        for human beauty in the Renaissance was considered to
        require light skin and blonde hair.

165   *nothing:* in no way

166   *To Cato's . . . Portia:* Cato's daughter, also named Portia,
        was married to Brutus, the Roman aristocrat. She had a
        reputation for beauty and wisdom.

170   *golden fleece:* the fabulous golden sheepskin that Jason, the
        Greek hero-adventurer, and his Argonauts brought from
        Colchis (a country on the Black Sea) back to Greece. In
        Elizabethan England, the fleece represented the success or
        fortune sought by sea-faring merchants. The use of "fleece"
        here points to both the beauty of Portia's hair and her wealth.

171   *seat:* home; *strand:* beach, shore

173   *means:* money

174   *rival:* equal

175   *presages:* predicts (with a sense of foreshadowing)

178   *commodity:* merchandise (to serve as a guarantee for a loan)

181   *rack'd:* stretched (as on the rack, an instrument of torture
        that stretched the victim's body over a wooden frame, pulling
        limbs out of joint)

182   *To furnish thee to Belmont:* to equip you for your journey to
        Belmont

184   *no question make:* am sure

185   *of my trust or for my sake:* either on the basis of my credit or
        as a personal favour to me

That which I owe is lost; but if you please
To shoot another arrow that self way
Which you did shoot the first, I do not doubt,
(As I will watch the aim) or to find both,   150
Or bring your latter hazard back again
And thankfully rest debtor for the first.
Antonio: You know me well, and herein spend but time
To wind about my love with circumstance;
And out of doubt you do me now more wrong   155
In making question of my uttermost
Than if you had made waste of all I have.
Then do but say to me what I should do
That in your knowledge may by me be done,
And I am prest unto it: therefore speak.   160
Bassanio: In Belmont is a lady richly left,
And she is fair, and, fairer than that word,
Of wondrous virtues: sometimes from her eyes
I did receive fair speechless messages:
Her name is Portia; nothing undervalu'd   165
To Cato's daughter, Brutus' Portia;
Nor is the wide world ignorant of her worth,
For the four winds blow in from every coast
Renowned suitors; and her sunny locks
Hang on her temples like a golden fleece;   170
Which makes her seat of Belmont Colchi's strand,
And many Jasons come in quest of her.
O my Antonio, had I but the means
To hold a rival place with one of them,
I have a mind presages me such thrift   175
That I should questionless be fortunate.
Antonio: Thou know'st that all my fortunes are at sea;
Neither have I money, nor commodity
To raise a present sum: therefore go forth,
Try what my credit can in Venice do: 180
That shall be rack'd, even to the uttermost,
To furnish thee to Belmont, to fair Portia.
Go, presently inquire, and so will I,
Where money is, and I no question make
To have it of my trust or for my sake.   *[Exeunt]*   185

Act 1, Scene 1: Activities

1. Shakespeare wrote his plays to be seen and heard, not to be read. When we read his lines silently, we miss the gestures, facial expressions, and vocal inflections that actors use to bring the lines to life. With a partner, use lines such as the following to investigate ways actors might interpret the script.

   a) Let me play the fool: . . .
      For this fool-gudgeon, this opinion. (lines 79–102)

      In this speech, Gratiano ridicules peevish old men and pompous fools by exaggerating their movements and voices. Act out the possibilities of this speech with your partner.

   b) In my school-days, when I had lost one shaft . . .
      And thankfully rest debtor for the first. (lines 140–152)

      Deliver this speech to your partner as you think Bassanio would do it. Remember that Bassanio tries to *demonstrate* his argument and to charm Antonio with a childlike sincerity.

   Record on audiotape or videotape your versions of your speeches for presentation and comparison. Compare your interpretations with those recorded by professionals. Note three similarities and three differences.

2. In the opening lines of the play (lines 8–40), Solanio and Salerio create images of ships at sea, of dangerous weather, and of silk and spice. These images all help to build an impression of business in medieval times.

   Suppose that you have been asked to update this play to modern times. Create a list of activities, places, and objects that would be appropriate to a play about business in today's world. Describe how your list reveals important changes in business practice since medieval times.

3. On the stage of life, Gratiano wishes to play the fool (lines 79–102). What recommendations does he make to one who might also like to play this role?

What role would you like to play in life? Write a brief description of the role and how it should be played. Here are some suggested roles: star athlete, scholar, politician, environmental activist.

4. Examine the speech in which Bassanio reveals his feelings about Portia (lines 161–176). Make a list of words and phrases that describe Bassanio as he appears to you in this speech. Take care to examine his reasons for pursuing Portia and look carefully at his reference to the story of Jason and the golden fleece.

   Review your list as you continue reading. Make additions and changes as you learn more about Bassanio.

5. Review Antonio's conversation with Bassanio (lines 119–185), making note of characteristics that contrast with Bassanio's personality.

   Begin with Antonio's choice of image (line 120) to determine differences in their values. Prepare a list of words and phrases that describe Antonio as he appears to you in this conversation. Change and add to this list as you learn more about Antonio.

6. How do you feel when somebody asks you for money, and how do you react? Assume that Antonio and Bassanio are living in the present. What circumstances might lead Bassanio to ask Antonio for money? Would the request change their relationship in any way? Discuss as a class.

For the next scene . . .

Recall a situation in which you felt you had no freedom of choice. How did you feel? What did you do?

19

Act 1, Scene 2

In this scene . . .

Portia and Nerissa, her maid and friend, discuss the
test of character that Portia's late father devised to find
a suitable husband for his daughter. According to her
father's will, each of Portia's suitors has to choose one
of three containers, or "caskets." The first casket is
made of gold, the second casket is made of silver, and
the third is made of lead. The man who is intelligent
enough to make the right choice will marry Portia. Portia
is clearly worried about the outcome of the lottery.
Nerissa entertains her by cataloguing the parade of
suitors who have already come to Belmont. Portia
ridicules them all. At the end of the scene, Nerissa
reminds Portia of her special interest in Bassanio, who
once visited Belmont.

1   *By my troth:* to tell the truth

5   *aught:* anything; *surfeit:* eat and drink to excess, overindulge

7   *mean:* insignificant (Compare the modern phrase "no mean feat.") *seated in the mean:* placed in the centre, between extremes. (Notice the pun on the word *mean*.)

8   *superfluity:* excess; *comes sooner by:* acquires, gets more quickly

9   *competency:* moderation

10   *sentences:* opinions, proverbs (here, advice)

13   *had been:* would have been

14   *divine:* preacher

18   *blood:* passions, emotions; *hot temper:* passionate, high-spirited, youthful temperament; *leaps o'er:* leaps over, ignores; *cold decree:* unfeeling

19   *hare:* rabbit

20   *meshes:* nets (In Elizabethan times, hares were hunted on foot with small-meshed nets.) *counsel:* advice

24   *curbed:* restricted, controlled (Notice Portia's pun on *will* in this same line.)

27-32   *Your father . . . rightly love:* Nerissa suggests that this lottery is not merely a game of chance.

Scene 2

Belmont. A room in Portia's house.
Enter Portia and Nerissa.

Portia: By my troth, Nerissa, my little body is aweary of
    this great world.
Nerissa: You would be, sweet madam, if your miseries were
    in the same abundance as your good fortunes are: and
    yet, for aught I see, they are as sick that surfeit with   5
    too much as they that starve with nothing. It is no
    mean happiness therefore, to be seated in the mean:
    superfluity comes sooner by white hairs, but
    competency lives longer.
Portia: Good sentences, and well pronounced.   10
Nerissa: They would be better if well followed.
Portia: If to do were as easy as to know what were good to
    do, chapels had been churches, and poor men's
    cottages princes' palaces. It is a good divine that follows
    his own instructions: I can easier teach twenty what   15
    were good to be done, than be one of the twenty to
    follow mine own teaching. The brain may devise laws
    for the blood, but a hot temper leaps o'er a cold decree:
    such a hare is madness (the youth), to skip o'er the
    meshes of good counsel (the cripple). But this reasoning   20
    is not in the fashion to choose me a husband. O me,
    the word 'choose'! I may neither choose who I would
    nor refuse who I dislike; so is the will of a living
    daughter curbed by the will of a dead father. Is it not
    hard, Nerissa, that I cannot choose one, nor refuse   25
    none?
Nerissa: Your father was ever virtuous, and holy men at
    their death have good inspirations; therefore, the lottery
    that he hath devised in these three chests of gold,
    silver, and lead, whereof who chooses his meaning   30

37   *level at:* try to guess

38   *Neapolitan:* from Naples, Italy

40   *appropriation:* compliment

41   *parts:* qualities

43   *smith:* blacksmith (What insult is Portia implying?)

44   *County Palatine:* Count Palatine was the title given to a nobleman who had complete right to rule his own territory within a state or kingdom.

45   *as who should say:* as much as to say; *And:* if

49   *unmannerly:* unsuitable, inappropriate

50   *death's-head:* skull

57   *he is . . . no man:* he has no personality; *throstle:* thrush, an English songbird

58   *a-capering:* dancing, leaping

61-62 *requite him:* return his love

70   *dumb-show:* performance in mime; *suited:* dressed

chooses you, will, no doubt, never be chosen by any
rightly but one who you shall rightly love. But what
warmth is there in your affection towards any of these
princely suitors that are already come?

Portia: I pray thee, over-name them, and as thou namest   35
them, I will describe them; and, according to my
description, level at my affection.

Nerissa: First there is the Neapolitan prince.

Portia: Ay, that's a colt indeed, for he doth nothing but
talk of his horse; and he makes it a great appropriation   40
to his own good parts that he can shoe him himself.
I am much afeard my lady his mother played false with
a smith.

Nerissa: Then is there the County Palatine.

Portia: He doth nothing but frown, as who should say, 'And   45
you will not have me, choose.' He hears merry tales,
and smiles not: I fear he will prove the weeping
philosopher when he grows old, being so full of
unmannerly sadness in his youth. I had rather be
married to a death's-head with a bone in his mouth than   50
to either of these. God defend me from these two!

Nerissa: How say you by the French lord, Monsieur Le Bon?

Portia: God made him, and therefore let him pass for a
man. In truth, I know it is a sin to be mocker; but, he!
why, he hath a horse better than the Neapolitan's, a   55
better bad habit of frowning than the Count Palatine;
he is every man in no man; if a throstle sing, he falls
straight a-capering; he will fence with his own shadow.
If I should marry him, I should marry twenty
husbands: if he would despise me, I would forgive   60
him, for if he loves me to madness, I shall never requite
him.

Nerissa: What say you, then, to Falconbridge, the young
baron of England?

Portia: You know I say nothing to him, for he understands   65
not me, nor I him: he hath neither Latin, French, nor
Italian; and you will come into the court and swear
that I have a poor pennyworth in the English. He is a
proper man's picture, but, alas! who can converse
with a dumb-show? How oddly he is suited! I think he   70

25

71   *doublet:* tunic. The nearest modern equivalent would be a tightly fitted suit jacket; *hose:* stockings, breeches

75-79   *That he hath . . . for another:* In Shakespeare's time, many people in Scotland and France shared a common dislike of the English. Indeed, Mary Queen of Scots was supported by many French people in her claim to the English throne.

76   *borrowed a box of the ear of:* was punched by

78   *surety:* supporter (guarantor of a loan)

78-79   *sealed under for another:* promised to repay (retaliate)

85-86   *And . . . fell:* if the worst should happen

86   *make shift:* make do, manage

90   *should refuse:* would be refusing

92   *Rhenish wine:* white wine from the Rhine Valley in Germany

95   *ere:* before

99   *suit:* courtship

101   *imposition:* command

102   *Sibylla:* a prophetess in ancient times, famous for her extreme old age as well as her predictions; *chaste:* pure, virginal

103   *Diana:* the Roman goddess of feminine virtue and purity

105-106 *dote on:* long for

bought his doublet in Italy, his round hose in France,
his bonnet in Germany, and his behaviour
everywhere.

Nerissa: What think you of the Scottish lord, his neighbour?

Portia: That he hath a neighbourly charity in him, for he   75
borrowed a box of the ear of the Englishman, and swore
he would pay him again when he was able: I think
the Frenchman became his surety and sealed under for
another.

Nerissa: How like you the young German, the Duke of   80
Saxony's nephew?

Portia: Very vilely in the morning, when he is sober, and
most vilely in the afternoon, when he is drunk: when
he is best, he is a little worse than a man, and when
he is worst, he is little better than a beast. And the   85
worst fall that ever fell, I hope I shall make shift to
go without him.

Nerissa: If he should offer to choose, and choose the right
casket, you should refuse to perform your father's
will, if you should refuse to accept him.   90

Portia: Therefore, for fear of the worst, I pray thee, set a
deep glass of Rhenish wine on the contrary casket,
for, if the devil be within and that temptation without,
I know he will choose it. I will do anything, Nerissa,
ere I will be married to a sponge.   95

Nerissa: You need not fear, lady, the having any of
these lords: they have acquainted me with their
determinations; which is, indeed, to return to their
home and to trouble you with no more suit, unless you
may be won by some other sort than your father's   100
imposition depending on the caskets.

Portia: If I live to be as old as Sibylla, I will die as chaste
as Diana, unless I be obtained by the manner of my
father's will. I am glad this parcel of wooers are so
reasonable, for there is not one among them but I dote   105
on his very absence, and I pray God grant them a fair
departure.

Nerissa: Do you not remember, lady, in your father's time,
a Venetian, a scholar and a soldier, that came hither
in company of the Marquis of Montferrat?   110

123   *condition:* character

124   *complexion of a devil:* In medieval and Renaissance times, the devil was thought to have dark skin. The association of black skin with evil is yet another indication of the prejudice of Shakespeare's day.

125   *shrive me:* hear my confession (as a priest would)

126   *Sirrah:* a term used by older persons to address men and boys of less authority, or with servants

Portia: Yes, yes: it was Bassanio—as I think so was he called.

Nerissa: True, madam: he of all the men that ever my foolish
    eyes looked upon, was the best deserving a fair lady.

Portia: I remember him well, and I remember him worthy
    of thy praise. 115

   [*Enter a Servant*]

    How now, what news?

Servant: The four strangers seek for you, madam, to take
    their leave; and there is a forerunner come from a fifth,
    the Prince of Morocco, who brings word the prince
    his master will be here tonight. 120

Portia: If I could bid the fifth welcome with so good heart
    as I can bid the other four farewell, I should be glad
    of his approach: if he have the condition of a saint
    and the complexion of a devil, I had rather he should
    shrive me than wive me. 125

   Come, Nerissa. [*To Attendant*] Sirrah, go before. Whiles
    we shut the gate upon one wooer, another knocks at
    the door.

                                 [*Exeunt*]

Act 1, Scene 2: Activities

1. If Nerissa and Portia were friends today, how would Nerissa express the piece of advice offered in lines 3–9? As Nerissa, write your advice either as a personal note to Portia or as it might appear in the advice column of a daily newspaper.

2. Portia feels trapped by her father's will. Adopting the role of her father, write the letter that he might have left her, explaining why the will is so strict and confining, or as Nerissa, write a note to justify her claim that the lottery was a "good inspiration."

3. Throughout this scene, what evidence can you find to suggest that Nerissa is a confidante and friend as well as a maid to Portia? Compare your findings with those of others in your class.

4. Prejudices are beliefs we hold about groups of people, especially racial, cultural, or national groups different from ourselves. Prejudices are like very dark glasses we wear when looking at individual members of these groups: they colour what we will see before we see it; they may even blind us totally to what is there. Often our prejudices are expressed through "stereotyping," the creating of exaggerated and superficial character types that contain all the expected faults of a target group.

    When Portia describes her suitors, she reduces each one to a comic stereotype of his nationality.

    a) With a partner, make a list of the six suitors described in this scene, and outline Portia's observations about each. As you review the list together, speculate upon the prejudices Shakespeare's audience might have held about French, German, and Scottish people.

    b) What aspects of Portia's descriptions of the suitors make you suspect that she is not accurately describing the European noblemen she had met, but is embellishing her descriptions to match her prejudices? (Consider, for example, whether a young German aristocrat would travel to Belmont only to be influenced by a glass of wine, or whether a French gentleman would dance to the song of a bird.) In a small group, generate a short list of the common features of Portia's speech (such as exaggeration, insult, biased selection of detail, uncomplimentary metaphor) that suggest she is "colouring" her descriptions.

c) In Portia's time, her stereotyping would have been considered normal and acceptable. We live in a different time, when most people believe that races and nationalities should live together with respect and understanding. On your own, write a letter explaining to a modern Portia the importance of rejecting stereotypes, even if they are intended to be funny.

d) What are the dangers of seeing people as stereotypes rather than as individuals? Are some forms of prejudice more dangerous than others? Record your thoughts and feelings, with examples, in your personal journal. Share your responses in a small group.

5. Portia has met each of her suitors only once. In pairs, write a modern script for Portia's interview with one of her suitors as it could have happened. In deciding what the suitor should say, pay attention to Portia's description of him, but remember her possible prejudices.

6. By the end of this scene, we suspect that Portia is in love with Bassanio. What obstacles can you see to their eventual marriage? In your notebook, list the obstacles and predict how they might be overcome.

For the next scene . . .

How do you know who your real friends are? What are the essential characteristics of a good friend? Would you be prepared to make commitments or take risks for a good friend? What risks would you be *un*willing to take for this friend?

Act 1, Scene 3

In this scene . . .

Bassanio and Antonio have come to borrow money from Shylock, the Jewish moneylender. Shylock can raise the amount required, but he seems unwilling to lend Antonio money because Antonio has insulted him so often in the past. Shylock and Antonio argue about the morality of lending money for profit, and it appears that they will not resolve their argument. Shylock eventually agrees to lend Antonio the money and, as a show of friendship, offers the loan interest-free. However, Shylock asks that Antonio promise to repay the loan with a pound of his flesh if he cannot provide the cash. Antonio immediately agrees despite Bassanio's protests. Antonio is sure that his ships will return a month before he has to repay the loan and that his life will not be in danger.

Shylock the Jew: The label attached to Shylock in the stage direction introduces the character as a stereotype. Shakespeare's audience immediately would have recognized Shylock as a Jew by his conventional stage costume and make-up. Their familiarity with the stereotype of the Jew and their own uninformed prejudice (Jews had been expelled from England at this time) would lead them to expect a "foreign" character who would display a set of values and a code of behaviour that they would find very different from, and inferior to, those of Elizabethan England.

1   *ducats:* gold coins, legal currency in Venice during the medieval and Renaissance periods. In modern terms, a ducat would be worth four or five dollars.

5   *bound:* legally responsible, as the guarantor of the loan

7   *stead:* help

13   *imputation:* suggestion, charge

16   *sufficient:* of adequate means or wealth; *his means are in supposition:* his money is tied up in uncertain investments

18   *Rialto:* the business district of Venice, named for the Rialto Bridge, on which many of the moneylenders ("bankers") and trading merchants conducted their business

20   *squandered:* scattered unwisely

23   *pirates:* (How would Shylock pronounce this word to make his pun?)

24   *notwithstanding:* nonetheless, in spite of this

25   *bond:* contract by which two parties are legally bound

Scene 3

Venice. A public place.
Enter Bassanio with Shylock
the Jew.

Shylock: Three thousand ducats; well.
Bassanio: Ay, sir, for three months.
Shylock: For three months; well.
Bassanio: For the which, as I told you, Antonio shall be
    bound.   5
Shylock: Antonio shall become bound; well.
Bassanio: May you stead me? Will you pleasure me? Shall
    I know your answer?
Shylock: Three thousand ducats, for three months, and
    Antonio bound.   10
Bassanio: Your answer to that?
Shylock: Antonio is a good man.
Bassanio: Have you heard any imputation to the contrary?
Shylock: Ho, no, no, no, no; my meaning in saying he is
    a good man is to have you understand me that he is   15
    sufficient. Yet his means are in supposition: he hath
    an argosy bound to Tripolis, another to the Indies; I
    understand moreover, upon the Rialto, he hath a
    third at Mexico, a fourth for England, and other
    ventures he hath squandered abroad. But ships are   20
    but boards, sailors but men: there be land-rats and
    water-rats, water-thieves and land-thieves—I mean
    pirates—and then there is the peril of waters, winds,
    and rocks. The man is, notwithstanding, sufficient.
    Three thousand ducats; I think I may take his bond.   25
Bassanio: Be assured you may.
Shylock: I will be assured I may; and, that I may be assured,
    I will bethink me. May I speak with Antonio?
Bassanio: If it please you to dine with us.

30-31   *to eat of . . . devil into:* to eat pork after Jesus cast devils into a herd of swine in order to restore a madman to sanity. (See *Mark* 5:1–13.) In fact, Jews are forbidden to eat pork by the laws of the Old Testament, written long before the time of Jesus.

37   *fawning publican:* cringing, flattering tax collector. In the Roman provinces, the collection of taxes was assigned to local people, who profited by squeezing money out of their own countrymen. The image of the publican may be one of the sources of the stereotype of the money-hungry Jew. Shylock would delight in applying this image to Antonio the Christian.

39   *simplicity:* stupidity

40   *gratis:* free (of interest). In 1258, a decree by Pope Alexander had barred Christians from charging interest on loans. Ironically, this provided an opportunity for some Jews, who were suffering under extreme conditions, to make a living. They could not move about freely, could not own land, and could not work for any government, but those who had managed to amass some capital were now sought out as the only "professional bankers" in Europe. As non-Christians, they were unaffected by the Pope's ban on interest.

41   *usance:* interest

42   *catch . . . upon the hip:* a metaphor from the sport of wrestling meaning to throw him off balance

43   *ancient grudge I bear him:* long-standing resentment I feel for him. The phrase suggests both the personal conflict between Shylock and Antonio and the religious tension between Christians and Jews.

46-47   *thrift . . . interest:* In this context, both words mean *profit.* Shylock, who lives, or "thrives," as a moneylender, prefers the word with more positive connotations. Antonio's term, *interest,* may imply "self-interest" or "greed."

47   *tribe:* the Jewish people

51   *gross:* total

54   *But soft!:* "Hang on! Wait a minute!"

55   *Rest you fair:* a polite greeting (Compare "God rest ye merry, gentlemen.")

57   *albeit:* although

58   *excess:* interest, profit

59   *ripe:* immediate; *wants:* needs

60   *possess'd:* informed, aware

61   *would:* want

Shylock: Yes, to smell pork; to eat of the habitation which   30
    your prophet the Nazarite conjured the devil into. I
    will buy with you, sell with you, talk with you, walk
    with you, and so following; but I will not eat with
    you, drink with you, nor pray with you. What news
    on the Rialto? Who is he comes here?   35
    [*Enter Antonio*]
Bassanio: This is Signior Antonio.
Shylock: [*Aside*] How like a fawning publican he looks!
    I hate him for he is a Christian;
    But more for that in low simplicity
    He lends out money gratis, and brings down   40
    The rate of usance here with us in Venice.
    If I can catch him once upon the hip,
    I will feed fat the ancient grudge I bear him.
    He hates our sacred nation, and he rails,
    Even there where merchants most do congregate,   45
    On me, my bargains, and my well-won thrift,
    Which he calls interest. Cursed be my tribe,
    If I forgive him!
Bassanio: Shylock, do you hear?
Shylock: I am debating of my present store,
    And, by the near guess of my memory,   50
    I cannot instantly raise up the gross
    Of full three thousand ducats. What of that?
    Tubal, a wealthy Hebrew of my tribe,
    Will furnish me. But soft! how many months
    Do you desire? [*To Antonio*] Rest you fair, good signior;   55
    Your worship was the last man in our mouths.
Antonio: Shylock, albeit I neither lend nor borrow
    By taking nor by giving of excess,
    Yet, to supply the ripe wants of my friend,
    I'll break a custom. [*To Bassanio*] Is he yet possess'd   60
    How much ye would?
Shylock: Ay, ay, three thousand ducats.
Antonio: And for three months.
Shylock: I had forgot; three months; you told me so.
    Well, then, your bond; and let me see—but here you;
    Methought you said, you neither lend nor borrow   65
    Upon advantage.

67   *Jacob:* grandson ("third possessor," line 70) of Abraham (Abram), the father of the Jewish people

69   *As his wise mother . . . behalf:* thanks to the intervention of his clever mother. Rebekah had devised a scheme that allowed Jacob to receive the blessing of his father, Isaac, in the place of his older half-brother, Esau (*Genesis* 27). Shylock's digression on the ancestry of his people leaves Antonio and Bassanio impatient.

73   *mark:* take note of

74   *compromis'd:* agreed

75   *eanlings:* newborn lambs; *pied:* spotted

76   *hire:* property; *rank:* ready for mating

78   *work of generation:* conception

79   *in the act:* taking place, underway

80   *pill'd:* peeled; *wands:* sticks. Jacob subscribed to the theory that coloured sticks set before the ewe would produce coloured lambs.

81   *in the doing . . . kind:* in imitation of the natural process

82   *fulsome:* abundant, lustful, rank (as above in line 76)

84   *Fall:* give birth to; *parti-colour'd:* multi-coloured

85   *thrive:* make a profit

87   *venture:* outcome; *serv'd for:* was not responsible for

90   *Was this inserted . . . good?:* Did you tell this story to justify lending money at interest?

92   *I make it breed:* By lending money at interest, Shylock makes more money.

94   *cite:* recite; *for his purpose:* to justify his own actions

98   *goodly:* a contraction of "good-like," suggesting the *appearance* of goodness

101   *beholding to you:* in your debt

102   *oft:* often

103   *rated:* berated, insulted

104   *usances:* usury, money-lending with interest

Antonio: I do never use it.
Shylock: When Jacob graz'd his uncle Laban's sheep—
  This Jacob from our holy Abram was,
  As his wise mother wrought in his behalf,
  The third possessor: ay, he was the third—   70
Antonio: And what of him? did he take interest?
Shylock: No, not take interest; not, as you would say,
  Directly interest: mark what Jacob did.
  When Laban and himself were compromis'd,
  That all the eanlings which were streak'd and pied   75
  Should fall as Jacob's hire, the ewes, being rank,
  In end of autumn turned to the rams;
  And, when the work of generation was
  Between these woolly breeders in the act,
  The skilful shepherd pill'd me certain wands,   80
  And, in the doing of the deed of kind,
  He stuck them up before the fulsome ewes,
  Who, then conceiving, did in eaning time
  Fall parti-colour'd lambs, and those were Jacob's.
  This was a way to thrive, and he was blest: 85
  And thrift is blessing, if men steal it not.
Antonio: This was a venture, sir, that Jacob serv'd for;
  A thing not in his power to bring to pass,
  But sway'd and fashion'd by the hand of heaven.
  Was this inserted to make interest good?   90
  Or is your gold and silver ewes and rams?
Shylock: I cannot tell; I make it breed as fast:
  But note me, signior.—
Antonio: Mark you this, Bassanio,
  The devil can cite Scripture for his purpose.
  An evil soul, producing holy witness,   95
  Is like a villain with a smiling cheek,
  A goodly apple rotten at the heart.
  O what a goodly outside falsehood hath!
Shylock: Three thousand ducats; 'tis a good round sum.
  Three months from twelve: then, let me see, the rate—   100
Antonio: Well, Shylock, shall we be beholding to you?
Shylock: Signior Antonio, many a time and oft
  In the Rialto you have rated me
  About my moneys and my usances:

105   *Still:* yet

107   *misbeliever:* literally, wrong-believer from Antonio's point of view, a heretic or non-Christian

108   *gaberdine:* loose upper garment. Though it was not the required practice in Venice, Jews elsewhere in Europe were restricted by law to a prescribed costume. As early as 1412, for example, Jews in Spain had to wear long robes over their clothes. The Jews had been expelled from England in 1290 and would not be readmitted until 1654, more than 50 years after the first staging of *The Merchant of Venice;* however, in Elizabethan theatres, there would have been a standard, recognizable Jew's costume.

111   *Go to:* C'mon! Get real! (This common Renaissance idiom is used to express disbelief.)

113   *void your rheum:* spit

114   *spurn:* kick; *stranger cur:* unfamiliar mongrel dog

115   *suit:* request, demand (What then is a *suitor?* a *lawsuit?*)

119   *in a bondman's key:* with the voice of a begging slave

120   *With bated breath:* hesitantly

129-130 *for when did friendship . . . friend:* for when did a friend make a profit on a loan to a friend? Christians considered money (*metal*) to be sterile (*barren*) because it was used as a means of exchange and never intended to be increased by interest (*breed*). The authority for this Christian doctrine is not the Bible, but the Greek philosopher Aristotle.

132   *break:* go broke (and fail to honour his bond); *with better face:* without appearing unfriendly (or, perhaps, simply *happily*)

133   *Exact:* collect

134   *would be:* would like to be

136   *doit:* small Dutch coin (a "penny")

137   *usance:* interest

140   *notary:* person authorized to draw up contracts; *seal:* Even today, a contract must bear a legal imprint or *seal* to be considered official.

141   *single bond:* a contract naming Antonio as the sole or single debtor to Shylock (Who then is *not* legally responsible for repayment?); *in a merry sport:* as a joke

Still have I borne it with a patient shrug, 105
For sufferance is the badge of all our tribe.
You call me misbeliever, cut-throat dog,
And spit upon my Jewish gaberdine,
And all for use of that which is mine own.
Well then, it now appears you need my help: 110
Go to then; you come to me, and you say,
'Shylock, we would have moneys:' you say so;
You, that did void your rheum upon my beard,
And foot me as you spurn a stranger cur
Over your threshold. Moneys is your suit. 115
What should I say to you? Should I not say,
'Hath a dog money? Is it possible
A cur can lend three thousand ducats?' or
Shall I bend low, and in a bondman's key,
With bated breath, and whispering humbleness, 120
Say this:
'Fair sir, you spat on me on Wednesday last;
You spurn'd me such a day; another time
You call'd me dog—and for these courtesies
I'll lend you thus much moneys'? 125
Antonio: I am as like to call thee so again,
To spit on thee again, to spurn thee too.
If thou wilt lend this money, lend it not
As to thy friends, for when did friendship take
A breed for barren metal of his friend? 130
But lend it rather to thine enemy;
Who if he break, thou may'st with better face
Exact the penalty.
Shylock: Why, look you, how you storm!
I would be friends with you, and have your love,
Forget the shames that you have stain'd me with, 135
Supply your present wants, and take no doit
Of usance for my moneys, and you'll not hear me:
This is kind I offer.
Bassanio: This were kindness.
Shylock: This kindness will I show.
Go with me to a notary, seal me there 140
Your single bond; and, in a merry sport,
If you repay me not on such a day,

144   *Express'd in the condition:* stated in the terms of the contract; *forfeit:* penalty

145   *Be nominated for:* be stated as; *equal:* exact

145-146 *pound Of your fair flesh:* Shylock's proposal, while unusual, is certainly not original. Although scholars have not been able to pinpoint the exact source of Shakespeare's idea, a great number and variety of European tales and stories feature such a penalty for default on a loan. (Eyes, ears, noses, and feet were also popular.) Roman law actually allowed several creditors to divide a debtor's body among themselves. Note, however, that Jewish law does *not* allow the taking of a debtor's life as punishment for default.

146   *fair:* light-skinned

148   *Content, in faith:* Indeed, I agree, I am happy.

151   *dwell in my necessity:* remain in need or debt

152   *forfeit:* have to pay

154   *return:* revenue from the merchandise his ships are carrying

157   *hard:* cruel; *suspect:* to be suspicious of

160   *exaction:* collection

162   *estimable:* valued

166   *I pray you wrong me not:* I beg you not to do me wrong (by misinterpreting my kindly motives).

170   *purse:* put into my purse; *straight:* immediately

171   *in the fearful guard:* under the doubtful protection

172   *unthrifty knave:* careless servant (a rascal)

173   *Hie thee:* hurry; *gentle:* kind. The words *gentle* and *Gentile* (non-Jewish) were frequently pronounced and spelled in the same way during Elizabethan times. This pun is used several times in the play by the Christian characters, usually to ridicule Shylock.

In such a place, such sum or sums as are
Express'd in the condition, let the forfeit
Be nominated for an equal pound   145
Of your fair flesh, to be cut off and taken
In what part of your body pleaseth me.
Antonio: Content, in faith: I'll seal to such a bond,
    And say there is much kindness in the Jew.
Bassanio: You shall not seal to such a bond for me: 150
    I'll rather dwell in my necessity.
Antonio: Why, fear not, man, I will not forfeit it:
    Within these two months, that's a month before
    This bond expires, I do expect return
    Of thrice three times the value of this bond.   155
Shylock: O father Abram, what these Christians are,
    Whose own hard dealings teaches them suspect
    The thoughts of others! Pray you, tell me this:
    If he should break his day, what should I gain
    By the exaction of the forfeiture?   160
    A pound of man's flesh, taken from a man,
    Is not so estimable, profitable neither,
    As flesh of muttons, beefs, or goats. I say,
    To buy his favour, I extend this friendship:
    If he will take it, so; if not, adieu;   165
    And, for my love, I pray you wrong me not.
Antonio: Yes, Shylock, I will seal unto this bond.
Shylock: Then meet me forthwith at the notary's;
    Give him direction for this merry bond.
    And I will go and purse the ducats straight,   170
    See to my house, left in the fearful guard
    Of an unthrifty knave, and presently
    I'll be with you.   [*Exit Shylock*]
Antonio: Hie thee, gentle Jew.
    The Hebrew will turn Christian: he grows kind.
Bassanio: I like not fair terms and a villain's mind.   175
Antonio: Come on: in this there can be no dismay;
    My ships come home a month before the day.
                                              [*Exeunt*]

Act 1, Scene 3: Activities

1. Carefully reread the opening lines of this scene (lines 1–35). Begin a list of descriptive words and phrases that outline your first impressions of Shylock. Note, for example, the careful deliberation of his opening lines and the extent of his knowledge of Antonio's business. What specific characteristics of Shylock's personality here suggest that he may be the antagonist or "villain" of the play?

   Remember that first impressions can often be misleading. Be prepared to change or add to your list of impressions of Shylock as you learn more about him in this scene and throughout the play.

2. An *aside* is a speech delivered by a character directly to the audience. Although other characters are present on stage, the audience understands that these characters are not supposed to hear the words of the speaker. Thus, an aside allows a character to reveal his or her innermost thoughts and feelings.

   Carefully reread Shylock's first aside (lines 37–48). Note how our simple view of Shylock as the "villain" becomes more complicated.

   With a partner, rehearse Shylock's speech for reading to the class or recording. Try to project all the different feelings Shylock has in his aside.

3. Antonio decides to make an exception to his own rule that he should never borrow money at interest (lines 57–60). Do you think his decision can be justified? Do you admire Antonio for placing more value on friendship than on rules of conduct? Discuss these two questions in a small group.

4. Antonio's speech on "a villain with a smiling cheek" (lines 93–98) is a warning against hypocrisy, that is, a warning against people who deliberately present false impressions of themselves. Imagine that you are the editor of Shakespeare's text and that this speech has been lost. Knowing what Shakespeare intended, how would you compose Antonio's speech in modern English? Share your version of the speech with a partner.

5. What is your reaction to Shylock's account of Antonio's behaviour toward him (lines 102–125)?

Complete either of the following activities:

a) If you have not been a victim of prejudice, imagine yourself in Shylock's position or in a modern-day situation in which you might be treated in a similar way. Record your thoughts and feelings in a personal journal entry.

OR

b) If you have been a victim of prejudice yourself, in what ways do you identify with Shylock's pain? Record your thoughts and feelings in a personal journal entry. If you are comfortable talking about your experience, share your thoughts and feelings with a trusted partner. (If you are the partner, ask questions and listen. Resist the temptation to give advice, unless you are asked for it.)

6. a) In the role of a Venetian lawyer, draw up the contract to be signed by Shylock and Antonio. Be sure that the exact terms and conditions are clearly stated.

b) Imagine that you are a local reporter. Write or videotape a news report on this outrageous contract. Provide specific and detailed information, including quotations from Bassanio as well as Antonio and Shylock.

7. Bassanio's final comment in this scene (line 175) uses the device of *foreshadowing*. In other words, his comment hints at events to follow. Using "Predictions" as your title, make a catalogue of all the possible events that might happen in the play. Compare lists with a partner.

For the next scene . . .

Why do people gamble? When they gamble, do people ever risk more than money? What role does luck play in gambling? What role does intelligence play in gambling?

Act 2, Scene 1

In this scene . . .

The Prince of Morocco, one of Portia's suitors, has arrived at Belmont. He boasts of his valour and physical courage, but he laments that these outstanding qualities can play no part in a contest controlled by luck. Portia warns the prince that the lottery has a penalty. If he chooses the wrong casket, he will have to swear never to marry.

2	*shadow'd livery:* dark uniform. Liveries are the uniforms worn by footmen, chauffeurs, and other types of servants. Morocco is using a metaphor to describe the colour of his skin. *burnish'd:* shining
3	*near bred:* closely related
4	*fairest:* (Is Morocco punning here?)
5	*Phoebus' fire:* the sun. Phoebus Apollo was the classical god of the sun.
6	*make incision:* cut ourselves
7	*reddest:* Traditionally, red blood symbolizes courage.
8	*aspect:* appearance
9	*fear'd:* frightened; *valiant:* brave
10	*best regarded:* most valued, of the highest reputation; *clime:* climate, country
11	*hue:* colour
13-14	*In terms of choice . . . maiden's eyes:* When I choose, I am hard to please, not influenced only by what appeals to my eyes.
15	*the lottery of my destiny:* the contest that controls my future or fate
16	*Bars:* denies
17	*scanted:* restricted
18	*hedg'd:* contained; *wit:* intelligence
18-19	*to yield myself His wife:* to become the wife of the man
20	*stood as fair:* another pun—would have had as fair a chance, or would be as attractive to me
24	*scimitar:* short curved sword
25	*Sophy:* Emperor of Persia
26	*Sultan Solyman:* famed commander of the Turkish forces that defeated Persia in 1535
27	*o'erstare:* overstare, outstare

Act 2, Scene 1

Belmont. A room in Portia's house.

Enter the Prince of Morocco, and his Followers; Portia and Nerissa.

Morocco: Mislike me not for my complexion,
   The shadow'd livery of the burnish'd sun,
   To whom I am a neighbour, and near bred.
   Bring me the fairest creature northward born,
   Where Phœbus' fire scarce thaws the icicles,   5
   And let us make incision for your love,
   To prove whose blood is reddest, his or mine.
   I tell thee, lady, this aspect of mine
   Hath fear'd the valiant: by my love, I swear
   The best regarded virgins of our clime   10
   Have lov'd it too: I would not change this hue,
   Except to steal your thoughts, my gentle queen.
Portia: In terms of choice I am not solely led
   By nice direction of a maiden's eyes;
   Besides, the lottery of my destiny   15
   Bars me the right of voluntary choosing:
   But if my father had not scanted me
   And hedg'd me by his wit, to yield myself
   His wife who wins me by that means I told you,
   Yourself renowned prince, then stood as fair   20
   As any corner I have look'd on yet
   For my affection.
Morocco: Even for that I thank you:
   Therefore, I pray you, lead me to the caskets
   To try my fortune. By this scimitar—
   That slew the Sophy, and a Persian prince   25
   That won three fields of Sultan Solyman—
   I would o'erstare the sternest eyes that look;
   Outbrave the heart most daring on the earth;
   Pluck the young sucking cubs from the she-bear;

32	*Lichas:* a servant of the heroic Hercules
33	*Which is the better man:* to see which is the better man
35	*Alcides:* Hercules, son of Alcaeus; *page:* servant (that is, Lichas)
42	*advis'd:* warned
44	*temple:* probably a small chapel within Portia's palace. There Morocco would take the oath referred to in lines 40–42.
45	*hazard:* chance, risk, gamble
46	*cursed'st:* most cursed

Yea, mock the lion when he roars for prey,   30
To win thee, lady. But, alas the while!
If Hercules and Lichas play at dice
Which is the better man, the greater throw
May turn by fortune from the weaker hand:
So is Alcides beaten by his page;   35
And so may I, blind fortune leading me,
Miss that which one unworthier may attain,
And die with grieving.
Portia: You must take your chance;
And either not attempt to choose at all,
Or swear before you choose, if you choose wrong,   40
Never to speak to lady afterward
In way of marriage: therefore be advis'd.
Morocco: Nor will not: come, bring me unto my chance.
Portia: First, forward to the temple: after dinner
Your hazard shall be made.   45
Morocco: Good fortune then!
To make me blest or cursed'st among men!   [*Exeunt*]

Act 2, Scene 1: Activities

1. What, if anything, does this scene contribute to the plot of the play? Assume you are the director of the play. In your notebook, explore the possible musical accompaniment and sound and visual effects you might add to this scene to ensure its success. Create a point-form list of music, sound effects, costumes, props, and lighting effects that reflect the choices that you might incorporate into this scene. Your list should include at least ten items and line references to the text.

   You might consider these stage directions that appear in early editions of the play: "Flourish of cornets. Enter Morocco, a tawny Moor all in white, and three or four followers, accordingly, with Portia, Nerissa, and their train."

2. Morocco's first line tells us that he fears he will not be treated fairly because of his race. Working in pairs, improvise either of the following scenarios:

   a) a conversation with a confidant before the meeting with Portia. What does he expect Portia's attitude to him will be, especially in view of his nobility and reputation? Why does he expect to encounter prejudice in Belmont, and how does he intend to combat it?

   OR

   b) a radio or television interview with the Prince of Morocco after his meeting with Portia. What were his impressions of Portia, and how does he plan to proceed? Why does he feel that the lottery is worth the risk?

   Make an audio or video recording of your scenario.

3. Contrast Portia's comment to Morocco (lines 20–22) with what she said to Nerissa at the end of Act 1, Scene 2 (lines 121–125). Is she lying to Morocco? What do these lines in combination tell us about Portia? Discuss Portia's behaviour in a small group, then summarize your own conclusions in a short letter to Portia, expressing your own opinion about her treatment of Morocco.

4. Prepare a costume design for either Portia or Morocco as they appear in this scene. Use the Internet and costume books from the library to research and validate your interpretation. Present your artwork to the class.

5. Using the list of *dramatis personae* that appears on page 5 of this text, draw a diagram of the relationships among the characters of the play. Be prepared to revise and add to your diagram as you learn more.

For the next scene . . .

Who are your favourite comedians and comic actors? How do they make you laugh? What are the talents, skills, or techniques of a good comedian or comic actor?

Act 2, Scene 2

In this scene . . .

Launcelot Gobbo has a dilemma: should he follow the moral advice of his conscience and stay with his master Shylock, or should he give in to his temptation to run away? He has heard that Bassanio is looking for servants and finally decides not to lose the opportunity for a new position. As he bolts from the stage, he bumps into his own father, Old Gobbo, who is so weak in sight that he does not recognize his son. Launcelot decides to use his father's blindness to amuse himself and the audience at his father's expense, but eventually he identifies himself. Old Gobbo has brought a present for Shylock as thanks for looking after his boy; Launcelot insists that the gift be saved for Bassanio, who now enters.

Bassanio is busy with preparations for his departure for Belmont. There are letters to be written and delivered, uniforms to be made for his new servants, torchbearers to be hired for a masquerade, and a farewell supper to be given for his Venetian friends. Bassanio is amused by Launcelot's antics and eventually does admit the clown to his service.

As Launcelot goes to take his leave of Shylock, Gratiano seeks and gains permission to accompany Bassanio to Belmont—with a promise not to "play the fool" (this is a direct quotation from the text) and ruin Bassanio's chances of success with Portia.

1   *serve:* assist

2   *fiend:* devil

6   *take heed:* take care and listen

9   *pack:* run away;

10   *Via!:* On your way!

10-11   *for the heavens:* for heaven's sake

13   *honest:* good

15-17   *my father . . . kind of taste:* Launcelot hints that his father
         was not faithful to his wife and had been intimate with other
         women.

20   *To be ruled by:* If I were ruled by

22   *God bless the mark:* Pardon me (for what I'm about to say).
         This self-blessing is a kind of apology to avoid bad luck or
         evil.

24   *saving your reverence:* begging your pardon. Launcelot is
         speaking here to the audience, many of whom would have
         pretended offence at his reference to the devil.

25   *incarnation:* incarnate, in the flesh

26   *in my conscience:* in my opinion

Scene 2

Venice. The street outside Shylock's house.

Enter Launcelot Gobbo.

Launcelot: Certainly my conscience will serve me to run from
this Jew my master. The fiend is at mine elbow, and
tempts me, saying to me, 'Gobbo, Launcelot Gobbo,
good Launcelot,' or 'good Gobbo,' or 'good Launcelot
Gobbo, use your legs, take the start, run away.' My   5
conscience says, 'No; take heed, honest Launcelot;
take heed, honest Gobbo;' or, as aforesaid, 'honest
Launcelot Gobbo; do not run; scorn running with thy
heels.' Well, the most courageous fiend bids me pack:
'*Via*!' says the fiend; 'away!' says the fiend; 'for the   10
heavens, rouse up a brave mind,' says the fiend, 'and
run.' Well, my conscience, hanging about the neck of
my heart, says very wisely to me, 'My honest friend
Launcelot, being an honest man's son,'—or rather an
honest woman's son, for, indeed, my father did   15
something smack, something grow to, he had a kind
of taste—well, my conscience says, 'Launcelot, budge
not.' 'Budge!' says the fiend. 'Budge not!' says my
conscience. 'Conscience,' say I, 'you counsel well;'
'Fiend,' say I, 'you counsel well.' To be ruled by my   20
conscience, I should stay with the Jew my master,
who (God bless the mark!) is a kind of devil; and, to
run away from the Jew, I should be ruled by the
fiend, who (saving your reverence) is the devil himself.
Certainly, the Jew is the very devil incarnation; and,   25
in my conscience, my conscience is but a kind of hard
conscience, to offer to counsel me to stay with the
Jew. The fiend gives the more friendly counsel:
I will run, fiend; my heels are at your commandment;
I will run.   30

34	*true-begotten:* fathered. In reality, Launcelot is Gobbo's true-begotten son!
35	*sand-blind:* half-blind; *high gravel-blind:* almost completely blind
36	*try confusions:* try to confuse (by playing tricks on him). However, Launcelot may mean *to try conclusions*, that is, to engage in a battle of wits.
40	*marry:* by the Virgin Mary, an exclamation of emphasis (in truth)
43	*sonties:* saints; *hit:* find
47	*raise the waters:* make him cry
50	*exceeding:* very
51	*well to live:* in good health
52	*a':* he
54	*Your worship's:* The term of respect indicates that Gobbo has still not recognized his son.
55	*ergo:* therefore (Latin) (Does Launcelot know the meaning of the word?)
57	*an't:* if it
59	*father:* The term was used generally to address an old man, not necessarily one's own father.
60-61	*the sisters three:* the Fates, three goddesses in classical mythology who control human destiny
66	*cudgel:* a short stick used as a weapon; *hovel-post:* supporting beam in a poor dwelling
68	*Alack:* alas, an expression of regret

[*Enter Old Gobbo, with a basket*]

Gobbo: Master young man, you; I pray you, which is the
    way to Master Jew's?

Launcelot: [*Aside*] O heavens! this is my true-begotten father,
    who, being more than sand-blind, high gravel-blind,   35
    knows me not: I will try confusions with him.

Gobbo: Master young gentleman, I pray you, which is the
    way to Master Jew's?

Launcelot: Turn up on your right hand at the next turning,
    but, at the next turning of all, on your left; marry,   40
    at the very next turning, turn of no hand, but turn
    down indirectly to the Jew's house.

Gobbo: By God's sonties, 'twill be a hard way to hit. Can
    you tell me whether one Launcelot, that dwells with
    him, dwell with him or no?   45

Launcelot: Talk you of young Master Launcelot? [*Aside*]
    Mark me now; now will I raise the waters. Talk you
    of young Master Launcelot?

Gobbo: No 'master', sir, but, a poor man's son; his father,
    though I say't, is an honest, exceeding poor man,   50
    and, God be thanked, well to live.

Launcelot: Well, let his father be what 'a will, we talk of
    young Master Launcelot.

Gobbo: Your worship's friend, and Launcelot, sir.

Launcelot: But I pray you, *ergo*, old man, *ergo*, I beseech   55
    you, talk you of young Master Launcelot?

Gobbo: Of Launcelot, an 't please your mastership.

Launcelot: Ergo, Master Launcelot. Talk not of Master
    Launcelot, father; for the young gentleman (according
    to fates and destinies and such odd sayings, the sisters   60
    three and such branches of learning) is, indeed,
    deceased; or, as you would say in plain terms, gone
    to heaven.

Gobbo: Marry, God forbid! the boy was the very staff of
    my age, my very prop.   65

Launcelot: [*Aside*] Do I look like a cudgel or a hovel-post,
    a staff or a prop? Do you know me, father?

Gobbo: Alack the day! I know you not, young gentleman:
    but I pray you, tell me, is my boy—God rest his soul!—
    alive or dead?   70

74-75   *it is a wise father . . . child:* In fact, the proverb says, "It is a wise child that knows his own father."

92   *fill-horse:* cart-horse. Many directors have Gobbo stroke the *back* of Launcelot's head during this speech.

97   *agree:* get along

99-100   *set up my rest:* made up my mind

101   *a very Jew:* a true Jew. Notice how Launcelot, too, reveals the prejudice of Shakespeare's England in its stereotyping of Jews.

102   *halter:* noose (to hang himself)

102-104   *I am famished . . . my ribs:* Rearrange the words to see what Launcelot really means.

103   *tell:* count

106   *liveries:* uniforms

Launcelot: Do you not know me, father?

Gobbo: Alack, sir, I am sand-blind; I know you not.

Launcelot: Nay, indeed, if you had your eyes, you might
    fail of the knowing me: it is a wise father that knows
    his own child. Well, old man, I will tell you news   75
    of your son. [*Kneels*] Give me your blessing: truth will
    come to light; murder cannot be hid long; a man's
    son may, but, in the end, truth will out.

Gobbo: Pray you, sir, stand up. I am sure you are not
    Launcelot, my boy.   80

Launcelot: Pray you, let's have no more fooling about it,
    but give me your blessing: I am Launcelot, your boy
    that was, your son that is, your child that shall be.

Gobbo: I cannot think you are my son.

Launcelot: I know not what I shall think of that; but I am   85
    Launcelot, the Jew's man, and I am sure Margery
    your wife is my mother.

Gobbo: Her name is Margery, indeed: I'll be sworn, if thou
    be Launcelot, thou art mine own flesh and blood.
    Lord worshipped might he be! what a beard hast thou   90
    got! thou hast got more hair on thy chin than Dobbin
    my fill-horse has on his tail.

Launcelot: It should seem then that Dobbin's tail grows
    backward: I am sure he had more hair of his tail than
    I have of my face, when I last saw him.   95

Gobbo: Lord, how art thou changed! How dost thou and
    thy master agree? I have brought him a present. How
    'gree you now?

Launcelot: Well, well: but, for mine own part, as I have set
    up my rest to run away, so I will not rest till I have   100
    run some ground. My master's a very Jew: give him
    a present? give him a halter! I am famished in his
    service; you may tell every finger I have with my ribs.
    Father, I am glad you are come: give me your present
    to one Master Bassanio, who, indeed, gives rare new   105
    liveries. If I serve not him, I will run as far as God
    has any ground. O rare fortune! here comes the man:
    to him, father; for I am a Jew, if I serve the Jew any
    longer.

[*Enter Bassanio, with Leonardo, and other Servants*]

110   *You may do so:* Bassanio is already in conversation with Leonardo when he enters; *let it be so hasted that:* hurry so that

112   *put the liveries to making:* arrange for the making of the uniforms

113   *anon:* at once

116   *Gramercy!:* Many thanks! (a corruption of the French *grand merci*); *wouldst thou aught:* Do you want anything?

120   *infection:* Gobbo means *affection* (desire, wish)

125   *scarce:* hardly; *cater-cousins:* good friends

128   *fruitify:* Launcelot means *specify, notify,* or *certify*

131   *impertinent:* Launcelot means *pertinent* (relevant)

137   *defect:* Gobbo means *effect* (point)
138   *suit:* request

140   *preferr'd:* recommended; *preferment:* promotion

143-145 *The old proverb . . . hath 'enough':* The old Scottish proverb is "The grace of God is gear enough," which means that the blessing of God is all one needs (the only *gear* or equipment one needs). Launcelot *parts* or divides the proverb, the first half going to Bassanio and the second half to Shylock.

147-148 *inquire My lodging out:* go to my house

Bassanio: You may do so; but let it be so hasted that supper   110
    be ready at the farthest by five of the clock. See these
    letters delivered; put the liveries to making; and
    desire Gratiano to come anon to my lodging.

                                                    [*Exit a Servant*]

Launcelot: To him, father.
Gobbo: God bless your worship!   115
Bassanio: Gramercy! wouldst thou aught with me?
Gobbo: Here's my son, sir, a poor boy—
Launcelot: Not a poor boy, sir, but the rich Jew's man; that
    would, sir—as my father shall specify—
Gobbo: He hath a great infection, sir (as one would say) to   120
    serve—
Launcelot: Indeed, the short and the long is, I serve the
    Jew, and have a desire, as my father shall specify—
Gobbo: His master and he (saving your worship's
    reverence) are scarce cater-cousins.   125
Launcelot: To be brief, the very truth is that the Jew having
    done me wrong, doth cause me—as my father being, I
    hope, an old man, shall frutify unto you—
Gobbo: I have here a dish of doves that I would bestow upon
    your worship, and my suit is—   130
Launcelot: In very brief, the suit is impertinent to myself,
    as your worship shall know by this honest old man;
    and, though I say it, though old man, yet (poor man)
    my father.
Bassanio: One speak for both. What would you?   135
Launcelot: Serve you, sir.
Gobbo: That is the very defect of the matter, sir.
Bassanio: I know thee well; thou hast obtain'd thy suit:
    Shylock thy master spoke with me this day,
    And hath preferr'd thee, if it be preferment   140
    To leave a rich Jew's service, to become
    The follower of so poor a gentleman.
Launcelot: The old proverb is very well parted between my
    master Shylock and you, sir: you have 'the grace of
    God', sir, and he hath 'enough'.   145
Bassanio: Thou speak'st it well. Go, father, with thy son.
    Take leave of thy old master, and inquire
    My lodging out. [*To his Servants*] Give him a livery

149   *guarded:* decorated (with *guards* or bands of colour)

150   *service:* job (as a servant). Launcelot is being sarcastic.

150-151 *I have . . . head:* I have no powers of persuasion.

152   *table:* palm of the hand. In the following lines, Launcelot is pretending to read his palm in order to predict his future.

156   *coming-in:* revenue, income (from their dowries)

157   *'scape:* escape

160   *for this gear:* for giving me this equipment (that is, his new liveries)

161   *in the twinkling:* in an instant (the twinkling of an eye)

163   *bestow'd:* stowed away (in the hold of Bassanio's ship)

164   *feast:* give a feast

165   *best-esteem'd acquaintance:* favourite friends

166   *herein:* in this matter

170   *suit:* request

173   *rude:* rough, unsophisticated

174   *Parts:* qualities (of character); *become:* fit, suit

177   *liberal:* extravagant

178   *allay:* cool, calm down; *modesty:* moderation

179   *skipping:* boisterous

180   *misconster'd:* misconstrued, misunderstood

More guarded than his fellows': see it done.

Launcelot: Father, in. I cannot get a service, no! I have ne'er   150
    a tongue in my head. Well, [*Looking at his hand*] if
    any man in Italy have a fairer table which doth offer
    to swear upon a book, I shall have good fortune. Go to;
    here's a simple line of life: here's a small trifle of
    wives: alas! fifteen wives is nothing: eleven widows and   155
    nine maids is a simple coming-in for one man; and
    then to 'scape drowning thrice, and to be in peril of
    my life with the edge of a feather-bed; here are simple
    'scapes. Well, if Fortune be a woman, she's a good
    wench for this gear. Father, come; I'll take my leave   160
    of the Jew in the twinkling.
                [*Exeunt Launcelot and Old Gobbo*]

Bassanio: I pray thee, good Leonardo, think on this.
    These things being bought, and orderly bestow'd,
    Return in haste, for I do feast tonight
    My best-esteem'd acquaintance. Hie thee, go.   165

Leonardo: My best endeavours shall be done herein.
    [*Enter Gratiano*]

Gratiano: Where's your master?

Leonardo: Yonder, sir, he walks.
                            [*Exit*]

Gratiano: Signior Bassanio!

Bassanio: Gratiano!

Gratiano: I have a suit to you.   170

Bassanio: You have obtain'd it.

Gratiano: You must not deny me: I must go with you to
    Belmont.

Bassanio: Why, then you must. But hear thee, Gratiano;
    Thou art too wild, too rude, and bold of voice—
    Parts that become thee happily enough,
    And in such eyes as ours appear not faults—   175
    But where thou art not known, why, there they show
    Something too liberal. Pray thee, take pain
    To allay with some cold drops of modesty
    Thy skipping spirit, lest, through thy wild behaviour,
    I be misconster'd in the place I go to,   180
    And lose my hopes.

Gratiano: Signior Bassanio, hear me:

182   *sober habit:* a pun: conservative clothing of a nun or a religious order; restrained behaviour

184   *Wear:* carry

185   *saying:* being said

187   *Use all . . . civility:* do all the right things at the right time

188   *Like one . . . sad ostent:* like a person well practised in displays of seriousness. Gratiano is contradicting the role he outlined earlier in the play.

189   *grandam:* grandmother

190   *bearing:* behaviour

191   *bar:* do not include; *gauge:* judge, measure

If I do not put on a sober habit,
Talk with respect, and swear but now and then,
Wear prayer-books in my pocket, look demurely,
Nay more, while grace is saying, hood mine eyes   185
Thus with my hat, and sigh, and say 'amen',
Use all the observance of civility,
Like one well studied in a sad ostent
To please his grandam, never trust me more.
Bassanio: Well, we shall see your bearing.   190
Gratiano: Nay, but I bar tonight; you shall not gauge me
    By what we do tonight.
Bassanio: No, that were pity:
    I would entreat you rather to put on
    Your boldest suit of mirth, for we have friends
    That purpose merriment. But fare you well: 195
    I have some business.
Gratiano: And I must to Lorenzo and the rest;
    But we will visit you at supper-time.   [*Exeunt*]

Act 2, Scene 2: Activities

1. A *soliloquy* is a speech in which a character thinks aloud while alone on stage. Launcelot's soliloquy presents his moral dilemma in a comic way. In a small group, rewrite the soliloquy as a short play for three characters (Launcelot, His Conscience, and Temptation). Rehearse your new scene for presentation to the class.

   Be sure to explore methods of conveying humour through both words and actions.

2. With a partner, choose a section of the scene between Launcelot and Old Gobbo and prepare it for dramatic presentation. Emphasize both the verbal humour (puns and nonsense) and the actions that are essential to successful staging of the scene. Blindfold the actor who will play Old Gobbo to increase the dramatic tension in your rendition of this scene.

3. A *malapropism* is the unintentional and humorous misuse of a word in place of another word that it closely resembles in sound. The term is derived from Mrs. Malaprop, a character in a play written in the eighteenth century, who confused expressions such as "illiterate him" with "obliterate him."

   a) For each of the contemporary examples of malapropism below, select the misused word and determine the word that was intended:

   - Trespassers will be persecuted!

   - The bullet rickshawed off the wall and hit him in the leg.

   - He finished the race, dripping with inspiration.

   - I like all types of books, but particularly hysterical fiction.

   b) Review Launcelot's malapropisms in this scene, noting how the "wrong" word always conveys real meaning, however inappropriate and comical. In the role of Launcelot, write a letter to your mother, Margery, in which you tell of your new employment. Use as many malapropisms as you can. Read your letter to your classmates to test the success of your humour.

4. With a partner, discuss the ways in which Gratiano's humour is different from Launcelot's. Consider the degree to which each is aware of his own comic effects. Think also about the difference between laughing *at* and laughing *with* a character.

   Remember the comedians you thought of in response to the questions on page 53. Decide whether these comedians are more like Gratiano or Launcelot. Discuss your conclusions with those of other groups in the class.

5. What might be Gratiano's possible reasons for wanting to accompany Bassanio to Belmont? Are any of these possibilities substantiated by his words in Act 1, Scene 1, and Bassanio's concerns in this scene? Record your responses in a journal entry.

For the next scenes . . .

Why do you think some teenagers run away from home? Which, if any, of your suggested reasons seem reasonable or justifiable to you? How would you counsel a friend who was planning to run away?

Act 2, Scenes 3, 4, 5, and 6

In these scenes . . .

The next four scenes introduce another storyline to the play. Jessica, Shylock's daughter, takes advantage of Launcelot's new position with Bassanio to pass a message to Lorenzo, one of Bassanio's friends and her own secret lover.

Lorenzo, Gratiano, and their friends are planning the entertainment for Bassanio's farewell dinner when Launcelot brings Jessica's letter. Lorenzo reveals to Gratiano the plan of escape that Jessica has devised: the masquerade will provide a perfect opportunity for Jessica, disguised as a page boy, to become Lorenzo's torchbearer and for the lovers to escape together from Venice.

Meanwhile, Shylock learns from Launcelot about the evening's masquerade and orders Jessica to shut herself in the house and pay no attention to the parade in the streets.

Shortly after Shylock's departure, Lorenzo and his friends arrive. Jessica is embarrassed by her male disguise, but is quick to flee with the money and jewels she has stolen from her father.

Just as the masquerade gets underway, Antonio enters to announce that the winds have changed direction and that Bassanio is setting sail for Belmont without delay.

3   *tediousness:* boredom

10   *Adieu!:* Goodbye! *exhibit:* Launcelot probably means *inhibit*
       (prevent). However, it is possible that his word choice is
       accurate here! (Compare the difference in meaning between
       "Tears exhibit my tongue" and "Tears inhibit my tongue.")
11   *pagan:* non-believer (here, a non-Christian)
13   *something:* somewhat
16   *heinous:* horrible, hateful

19   *not to his manners:* not like him in actions
20   *strife:* conflict, struggle

Scene 3

Venice. The street outside Shylock's house.

Enter Jessica and Launcelot.

Jessica: I am sorry thou wilt leave my father so:
    Our house is hell, and thou, a merry devil,
    Didst rob it of some taste of tediousness.
    But fare thee well; there is a ducat for thee—
    And, Launcelot, soon at supper shalt thou see   5
    Lorenzo, who is thy new master's guest:
    Give him this letter—do it secretly.
    And so farewell: I would not have my father
    See me in talk with thee.
Launcelot: Adieu! tears exhibit my tongue. Most beautiful   10
    pagan, most sweet Jew! If a Christian do not play the
    knave and get thee, I am much deceived. But, adieu!
    these foolish drops do something drown my manly
    spirit: adieu!
Jessica: Farewell, good Launcelot.   *[Exit Launcelot]*   15
    Alack, what heinous sin is it in me
    To be asham'd to be my father's child!
    But though I am a daughter to his blood,
    I am not to his manners. O Lorenzo,
    If thou keep promise, I shall end this strife,   20
    Become a Christian, and thy loving wife.   *[Exit]*

5   *not spoke us yet of:* not yet hired

6   *quaintly order'd:* done in style

9   *furnish us:* get ready

10   *And:* if; *break up:* open (by breaking the seal)

12   *the hand:* the handwriting. Notice the pun on *hand* in line 14.

18   *sup:* dine

22   *masque:* masked ball or masquerade party, preceded by a torch-lit parade through the streets

23   *provided of:* supplied with

Scene 4

Venice. A street.

Enter Gratiano, Lorenzo, Salerio,
and Solanio.

Lorenzo: Nay, we will slink away in supper-time,
　　Disguise us at my lodging, and return
　　All in an hour.
Gratiano: We have not made good preparation.
Salerio: We have not spoke us yet of torch-bearers.　　　　5
Solanio: 'Tis vile unless it may be quaintly order'd,
　　And better, in my mind, not undertook.
Lorenzo: 'Tis now but four o'clock: we have two hours
　　To furnish us.
　　[*Enter Launcelot, with a letter*]
　　　　　　　　　Friend Launcelot, what's the news?
Launcelot: And it shall please you to break up this, it shall　　10
　　seem to signify.
Lorenzo: I know the hand: in faith, 'tis a fair hand;
　　And whiter than the paper it writ on
　　Is the fair hand that writ.
Gratiano:　　　　　　　　Love news, in faith.
Launcelot: By your leave, sir.　　　　　　　　15
Lorenzo: Whither goest thou?
Launcelot: Marry, sir, to bid my old master, the Jew, to
　　sup tonight with my new master, the Christian.
Lorenzo: Hold here, take this: tell gentle Jessica
　　I will not fail her; speak it privately.　　　　20
　　Go, gentlemen,　　　　　　　　[*Exit Launcelot*]
　　Will you prepare you for this masque tonight?
　　I am provided of a torch-bearer.
Salerio: Ay, marry, I'll be gone about it straight.
Solanio: And so will I.　　　　　　　　25

29   *directed:* instructed

31   *furnish'd:* supplied

32   *page's suit:* costume of a young male servant

35   *foot:* path

36   *she:* misfortune (Although there is no capitalization, misfortune is personified here.)

37   *she is issue to:* Jessica is the child of; *faithless:* unbelieving because he is not a Christian. Of course, Shylock has a faith of his own.

38   *peruse:* look over

Lorenzo: Meet me and Gratiano
  At Gratiano's lodging some hour hence.
Salerio: 'Tis good we do so.
                         [*Exeunt Salerio and Solanio*]
Gratiano: Was not that letter from fair Jessica?
Lorenzo: I must needs tell thee all. She hath directed
  How I shall take her from her father's house;   30
  What gold and jewels she is furnish'd with;
  What page's suit she hath in readiness.
  If e'er the Jew her father come to heaven,
  It will be for his gentle daughter's sake;
  And never dare misfortune cross her foot,   35
  Unless she do it under this excuse,
  That she is issue to a faithless Jew.
  Come, go with me: peruse this as thou goest.
  Fair Jessica shall be my torch-bearer.   [*Exeunt*]

2   *of:* between

3   *What, Jessica:* Shylock calls to his daughter as he speaks with Launcelot; *gormandize:* overeat

5   *rend apparel out:* wear holes in your clothes

7   *bids:* asks

8   *wont:* accustomed, in the habit

12   *wherefore:* why

15   *prodigal:* wasteful

16   *Look to:* look after, take care of; *right loath:* very reluctant

17   *rest:* peace of mind

20   *reproach:* (What word does Launcelot mean? What is the irony of his malapropism?)

22   *conspired:* plotted

22-27   As soon as he lets slip the fact that Lorenzo and Bassanio have been plotting, Launcelot immediately tries to cover his revelation with nonsense. He also may be mocking Shylock's belief in dreams as omens to predict the future.

Scene 5

Venice. The street outside
Shylock's house.
Enter Shylock and Launcelot.

Shylock: Well, thou shalt see, thy eyes shall be thy judge
 The difference of old Shylock and Bassanio—
 What, Jessica!—thou shalt not gormandize
 As thou hast done with me—What, Jessica!—
 And sleep and snore, and rend apparel out—   5
 Why, Jessica, I say!
Launcelot: Why, Jessica!
Shylock: Who bids thee call? I do not bid thee call.
Launcelot: Your worship was wont to tell me that I could
  do nothing without bidding.
 [*Enter Jessica*]
Jessica: Call you? What is your will?   10
Shylock: I am bid forth to supper, Jessica;
 There are my keys. But wherefore should I go?
 I am not bid for love: they flatter me.
 But yet I'll go in hate, to feed upon
 The prodigal Christian. Jessica, my girl,   15
 Look to my house. I am right loath to go:
 There is some ill a-brewing towards my rest,
 For I did dream of money-bags tonight.
Launcelot: I beseech you, sir, go: my young master doth
  expect your reproach.   20
Shylock: So do I his.
Launcelot: And they have conspired together—I will not
  say you shall see a masque; but if you do, then it was
  not for nothing that my nose fell a-bleeding on Black
  Monday last, at six o'clock i' the morning, falling out   25
  that year on Ash Wednesday was four year in th'
  afternoon.

30   *wry-neck'd fife:* the fife is a wooden flute that is played sideways so that the player must hold his neck and head in a twisted (*wry*) position

31   *casements:* windows

33   *varnish'd:* wearing painted masks

34   *stop:* block up

35   *shallow foppery:* trivial foolishness

36   *sober:* serious; *By Jacob's staff:* Shylock's oath appropriately recalls the "success story" of his ancestor Jacob (*Genesis* 32:10) who embarked on a journey with only a staff and returned an affluent man.

43   *eye:* look or vigilance (Launcelot advises Jessica to "be on the lookout" for Lorenzo in disguise.)

44   *Hagar's offspring:* Ishmael, the illegitimate son of Abraham and Hagar, the Gentile slave of Abraham's wife (*Genesis* 21:9). Traditionally, Ishmael represents the outcast. This is meant as an insult to Launcelot.

46   *patch:* clown (who wears patched clothing); *kind:* good, decent

48   *drones:* male bees who do not work

54   *'Fast bind, fast find':* (Work out the meaning of this old saying, remembering that *fast* means tight or secure as well as quick.)

56   *if my fortune . . . cross'd:* if I am not unlucky

Shylock: What, are there masques? Here you me, Jessica:
    Lock up my doors, and when you hear the drum
    And the vile squealing of the wry-neck'd fife,   30
    Clamber not you up to the casements then,
    Nor thrust your head into the public street
    To gaze on Christian fools with varnish'd faces,
    But stop my house's ears—I mean my casements—
    Let not the sound of shallow foppery enter   35
    My sober house. By Jacob's staff I swear
    I have no mind of feasting forth tonight;
    But I will go. Go you before me, sirrah;
    Say I will come.
Launcelot: I will go before, sir. Mistress, look out at window,   40
    for all this:

    There will come a Christian by,
    Will be worth a Jewess' eye.

                       [*Exit Launcelot*]
Shylock: What says that fool of Hagar's offspring, ha?
Jessica: His words were, 'Farewell, mistress'; nothing else.   45
Shylock: The patch is kind enough, but a huge feeder;
    Snail-slow in profit, and he sleeps by day
    More than the wild cat: drones hive not with me;
    Therefore I part with him, and part with him
    To one that I would have him help to waste   50
    His borrow'd purse. Well, Jessica, go in—
    Perhaps I will return immediately—
    Do as I bid you; shut doors after you:
    'Fast bind, fast find',
    A proverb never stale in thrifty mind.   [*Exit*]   55
Jessica: Farewell; and if my fortune be not cross'd,
    I have a father, you a daughter, lost.   [*Exit*]

1	*penthouse:* balcony or second-storey porch
2	*make stand:* wait (for him)
3	*out-dwells his hour:* is late
5	*Venus' pigeons:* The chariot of Venus, Roman goddess of love, was pulled by doves.
5-7	*O ten times . . . unforfeited:* Gratiano and Salerio mock Lorenzo for being late. They suggest that, once a lover has received a commitment, he is no longer as careful or anxious about his behaviour.
8-19	*That ever holds . . . by the strumpet wind:* Gratiano offers three further examples of our habit of beginning something with more enthusiasm than we finish.
11	*unbated:* unabated, equal
14	*a younger or a prodigal:* In the parable, the prodigal son was the younger son (*Luke* 15: 11–32).
15	*scarfed bark:* ship decorated with flags and bunting (perhaps for its maiden voyage)
16	*strumpet:* faithless, fickle (in a sexual sense) (When the prodigal sets sail, he is favoured by the wind; on his return journey, the wind batters and abuses him.)
21	*abode:* delay
24	*watch:* stand guard

Scene 6

Venice. The street outside
Shylock's house.

Enter Gratiano and Salerio dressed
as masquers.

Gratiano: This is the penthouse under which Lorenzo
  Desir'd us to make stand.
Salerio: His hour is almost past.
Gratiano: And it is marvel he out-dwells his hour,
  For lovers ever run before the clock.
Salerio: O ten times faster Venus' pigeons fly   5
  To seal love's bonds new-made, than they are wont
  To keep obliged faith unforfeited!
Gratiano: That ever holds: who riseth from a feast
  With that keen appetite that he sits down?
  Where is the horse that doth untread again   10
  His tedious measures with the unbated fire
  That he did pace them first? All things that are,
  Are with more spirit chased than enjoy'd.
  How like a younger or a prodigal
  The scarfed bark puts from her native bay,   15
  Hugg'd and embraced by the strumpet wind!
  How like the prodigal doth she return,
  With over-weather'd ribs and ragged sails,
  Lean, rent, and beggar'd by the strumpet wind!
  [*Enter Lorenzo*]
Salerio: Here comes Lorenzo: more of this hereafter.   20
Lorenzo: Sweet friends, your patience for my long abode;
  Not I but my affairs have made you wait:
  When you shall please to play the thieves for wives,
  I'll watch as long for you then. Approach;
  Here dwells my father Jew. Ho! who's within?   25

27   *Albeit:* although; *tongue:* voice

33   *casket:* small chest; *pains:* trouble

35   *exchange:* change (of clothing—and gender!)

37   *pretty:* This word has a great many meanings. Here, it probably means *fine* in an ironic sense. Compare the contemporary expression "A fine mess we're in!"

38   *Cupid:* the Roman god of love, son of Venus, always appearing as an angelic child armed with a bow and arrow

42   *light:* obvious, evident (and also, foolish) (There may be some implication of immodesty as well.)

43   *'tis an office of discovery:* torch-bearing is a duty that reveals or lights up

44   *obscur'd:* darkened, hidden. In the next line, Lorenzo takes the meaning as *disguised.*

45   *garnish:* costume

47   *close:* dark and secret; *doth play the runaway:* is passing quickly (Why is the metaphor an appropriate one in this scene?)

48   *stay'd:* waited

49   *fast:* secure; *gild:* furnish (literally, decorate with gold)

51   *by my hood:* a mild oath of obscure origin, like "upon my word"; *gentle:* notice again the pun on *Gentile*

52   *Beshrew me:* curse me (another mild oath)

[*Enter Jessica on the balcony, dressed as a boy.*]

Jessica: Who are you? Tell me, for more certainty,
    Albeit I'll swear that I do know your tongue.

Lorenzo: Lorenzo, and thy love.

Jessica: Lorenzo, certain; and my love indeed,
    For who love I so much? And now who knows   30
    But you, Lorenzo, whether I am yours?

Lorenzo: Heaven and thy thoughts are witness that thou
    art.

Jessica: Here, catch this casket; it is worth the pains.
    I am glad 'tis night, you do not look on me,
    For I am much asham'd of my exchange: 35
    But love is blind, and lovers cannot see
    The pretty follies that themselves commit;
    For if they could, Cupid himself would blush
    To see me thus transformed to a boy.

Lorenzo: Descend, for you must be my torch-bearer.   40

Jessica: What! must I hold a candle to my shames?
    They in themselves, good sooth, are too too light.
    Why, 'tis an office of discovery, love,
    And I should be obscur'd.

Lorenzo: So are you, sweet,
    Even in the lovely garnish of a boy,   45
    But come at once;
    For the close night doth play the runaway,
    And we are stay'd for at Bassanio's feast.

Jessica: I will make fast the doors, and gild myself
    With some more ducats, and be with you straight.   50
                      [*Exit above*]

Gratiano: Now, by my hood, a gentle, and no Jew.

Lorenzo: Beshrew me, but I love her heartily;
    For she is wise, if I can judge of her;
    And fair she is, if that mine eyes be true;
    And true she is, as she hath prov'd herself;   55
    And therefore, like herself, wise, fair, and true,
    Shall she be placed in my constant soul.
    [*Enter Jessica*]
    What, art thou come? On, gentlemen; away!
    Our masquing mates by this time for us stay.
                  [*Exeunt, except Gratiano*]

64   *is come about:* has changed direction (The expression is
       associated with sailing.)

[*Enter Antonio.*]
Antonio: Who's there?   60
Gratiano: Signior Antonio!
Antonio: Fie, fie, Gratiano! where are all the rest?
    'Tis nine o'clock; our friends all stay for you.
    No masque tonight: the wind is come about;
    Bassanio presently will go aboard: 65
    I have sent twenty out to seek for you.
Gratiano: I am glad on't: I desire no more delight
    Than to be under sail and gone tonight.   [*Exeunt*]

Act 2, Scenes 3, 4, 5, and 6: Activities

1. Return to the question from Act 2, Scene 1, Activity 5, and your diagram of the relationships among the *dramatis personae.* Update your diagram with new information.

2. List the ways in which the addition of a love affair between Lorenzo and Jessica might complicate the situation for Antonio and Bassanio. Consider *all* the possibilities. Compare your list with that of a partner.

3. In these scenes, the audience's relationship to Shylock becomes more complicated. In a small group, compare and discuss your attitudes to him. How are we led to dislike him *and* to sympathize with him simultaneously? Which emotion predominates in your own reading of these scenes?

   Update the list of descriptive words and phrases that you began in Act 1, and try to reach a group consensus about the nature of Shylock's character at this point in the play.

4. Compare Launcelot's and Shylock's versions of the history of Launcelot's service in Shylock's house. (For Launcelot's side of the story, you will need to review Act 2, Scene 2.)

   If you were directing this play, whose side of the issue would you want the audience to take? Why? How could casting affect the audience's sympathy for Launcelot? Consider obvious physical features as well as Launcelot's attitude, gestures, and voice. How would you cast the part of Launcelot to help the audience to decide who was telling the truth? Record your ideas in a director's log, and compare notes with others in the class.

5. Make a list of all Bassanio's possible motives for inviting Shylock to dinner. Be sure to find all the clues provided in the text. Which clues might lead you to believe that Bassanio is an "accomplice" in the elopement plot?

   Now, write a journal entry as Bassanio, revealing your true motivation.

6. Debate in parliamentary style: Be it resolved that Shylock shows himself to be a caring and loving father in Scene 5.

7. Discuss with a partner, in a small group, or as a class:

   a) Is Jessica right to elope with Lorenzo?

   b) Is she justified in taking money and jewels with her?

   How do you think Shakespeare's audience would have responded to Jessica's actions? Do you think they would have found irony in Lorenzo's speech praising Jessica (Scene 6, lines 52–57)? Would a modern audience react differently? Why?

8. *Dramatic irony* occurs frequently in Shakespeare's plays. It often springs from the contrast between the knowledge of the audience and the ignorance of a character or characters. In these scenes, there is dramatic irony in Shylock's leaving his house and possessions in Jessica's care. Explain the dramatic irony in these scenes.

   What types of television programs and films appear to provide the richest sources of dramatic irony? What effects does dramatic irony have on the audience? As a short research project, survey and report on examples of dramatic irony in an average week's television viewing.

For the next scene . . .

What is the possession you value most? Why do you value it? Is its value obvious to the eye? If not, how would others come to know its importance to you?

Act 2, Scene 7

In this scene . . .

In Belmont, the Prince of Morocco is ready to choose
one of the three caskets. Although he believes in his
own worthiness as a suitor and feels that he deserves to
have Portia on the basis of his own merits, he decides
to submit himself to the "game of chance" her father
has devised. He reads aloud the inscription on each of
the three caskets and tries to puzzle out their meanings.

1	*discover:* reveal
2	*several:* different

9 *hazard:* venture, risk

12 *I am yours withal:* I and all I own are yours.

14 *back again:* in reverse order

19 *fair advantages:* reasonable gains, worthwhile rewards
20 *stoops not . . . dross:* does not lower itself to worthless displays. (Dross is the scum that forms on the surface of molten metal.)
21 *aught:* anything
22 *virgin hue:* unblemished sheen or polish
25 *weigh:* consider, estimate; *even:* impartial, unbiased
26 *be'st rated:* be evaluated

Scene 7

Belmont. A room in Portia's house.

*Enter Portia, with the
Prince of Morocco,
and their Servants.*

Portia: Go, draw aside the curtains, and discover
  The several caskets to this noble prince.
                     [*The curtains are drawn back*]
  Now make your choice.
Morocco: The first, of gold, who this inscription bears:
  '*Who chooseth me shall gain what many men desire*'.   5
  The second, silver, which this promise carries:
  '*Who chooseth me shall get as much as he deserves*'.
  This third, dull lead, with warning all as blunt:
  '*Who chooseth me must give and hazard all he hath*'.
  How shall I know if I do choose the right?   10
Portia: The one of them contains my picture, prince:
  If you choose that, then I am yours withal.
Morocco: Some god direct my judgment! Let me see:
  I will survey th' inscriptions back again:
  What says this leaden casket?   15
  '*Who chooseth me must give and hazard all he hath*'.
  Must give! For what? for lead? hazard for lead?
  This casket threatens. Men that hazard all
  Do it in hope of fair advantages:
  A golden mind stoops not to shows of dross;   20
  I'll then nor give nor hazard aught for lead.
  What says the silver with her virgin hue?
  '*Who chooseth me shall get as much as he deserves*'.
  As much as he deserves! Pause there, Morocco,
  And weigh thy value with an even hand.   25
  If thou be'st rated by thy estimation,

29-30   *to be afeard . . . disabling of myself:* to be afraid to choose what I deserve is really to undervalue my worth and to discredit myself

36   *grav'd:* engraved

40   *shrine:* The relics or remains of saints were encased in small caskets or monuments (*shrines*). The saint was often sculpted or painted on the outside of the shrine and kissed for reverence.

41   *Hyrcanian deserts:* wild uninhabited lands to the south of the Caspian Sea in Asia Minor; *vasty wilds:* vast deserted lands

42   *throughfares:* thoroughfares, highways

44-45   *The watery kingdom . . . face of heaven:* the oceans and seas, whose waves reach up to touch the sky

45   *bar:* obstacle

46   *foreign spirits:* suitors from abroad

47   *As o'er a brook:* as if they had only to cross a stream

49   *Is 't like:* is it likely

50-51   *it were too gross . . . obscure grave:* Lead would be too vulgar even as a funeral casket to hold (*rib*) her wrapped body in the dark grave. A *cerecloth* is the waxed cloth or shroud in which a corpse is wrapped.

52   *immur'd:* walled in, contained

53   *tried:* tested (and found to be pure)

54-55   *Never so rich . . . gold:* (To what is Morocco comparing Portia in this compliment?)

57   *insculp'd upon:* engraved on the surface of the coin. The "angel" was a gold coin in circulation at this time; it featured the victory of the archangel Michael over a dragon.

60   *thrive:* succeed

61   *form:* likeness, portrait

63   *A carrion Death:* a skull

Thou dost deserve enough; and yet enough
May not extend so far as to the lady:
And yet to be afeard of my deserving
Were but a weak disabling of myself. 30
As much as I deserve! Why, that's the lady:
I do in birth deserve her, and in fortunes,
In graces, and in qualities of breeding;
But more than these, in love I do deserve.
What if I stray'd no further, but chose here? 35
Let's see once more this saying grav'd in gold:
'Who chooseth me shall gain what many men desire'.
Why, that's the lady: all the world desires her;
From the four corners of the earth they come,
To kiss this shrine, this mortal breathing saint: 40
The Hyrcanian deserts and the vasty wilds
Of wide Arabia are as throughfares now
For princes to come view fair Portia:
The watery kingdom, whose ambitious head
Spits in the face of heaven, is no bar 45
To stop the foreign spirits, but they come,
As o'er a brook, to see fair Portia.
One of these three contains her heavenly picture.
Is 't like that lead contains her? 'Twere damnation
To think so base a thought: it were too gross 50
To rib her cerecloth in the obscure grave.
Or shall I think in silver she's immur'd,
Being ten times undervalu'd to tried gold?
O sinful thought! Never so rich a gem
Was set in worse than gold. They have in England 55
A coin that bears the figure of an angel
Stamp'd in gold, but that's insculp'd upon;
But here an angel in a golden bed
Lies all within. Deliver me the key:
Here do I choose, and thrive I as I may! 60
Portia: There, take it, prince; and if my form lie there,
　　Then I am yours.
　　　　　　　　　[He unlocks the golden casket]
Morocco: 　　　　O hell! what have we here?
　　A carrion Death, within whose empty eye
　　There is a written scroll. I'll read the writing.

65   *glisters:* sparkles, glistens

69   *infold:* contain

71   *old:* (What does "old" in judgment mean?)
72   *had not been inscroll'd:* would not have been written on this
       scroll
73   *Cold:* dead

77   *tedious:* long, lengthy

79   *complexion:* It seems almost impossible to overlook Portia's
       prejudice here. The word *complexion* can mean personality
       as well as colour (of the skin). Which meaning does Portia
       intend? Or does she intend a pun?

All that glisters is not gold; 65
Often have you heard that told:
Many a man his life hath sold
But my outside to behold:
Gilded tombs do worms infold.
Had you been as wise as bold, 70
Young in limbs, in judgment old,
Your answer had not been inscroll'd.
Fare you well, your suit is cold.

Cold, indeed; and labour lost:
Then farewell heat, and welcome, frost! 75
Portia, adieu. I have too griev'd a heart
To take a tedious leave: thus losers part.
                    [*Exit with his Servants*]
Portia: A gentle riddance. Draw the curtains: go. Let all of his
    complexion choose me so.   [*Exeunt*]

Act 2, Scene 7: Activities

1. The spectacle of the room, the three chests, and the costumes could be used to reinforce the main theme of this scene. With a partner, create two different set and costume designs for the scene, and be prepared to explain to the class how your changes would affect the audience's understanding of the scene.

2. As the official scribe (record-keeper) of the court of Morocco, write your account of the Prince's attempt and failure to solve the riddle of the caskets and their inscriptions. Outline the reasoning that led the Prince to his choice.

   As a biased reporter, you could conclude with a defence of your Prince's argument.

   You may wish to prepare and deliver your report in the role of a modern sports commentator or as a tabloid "gossip" columnist.

3. Consider again Morocco's complaint about the lottery, voiced earlier in the play:

   If Hercules and Lichas play at dice
   Which is the better man, the greater throw
   May turn by fortune from the weaker hand . . .
   (Act 2, Scene 1, lines 32–34)

   With a partner or in a small group, assess the validity of Morocco's comparison of the lottery to a game of chance. How might Portia's father have defended his lottery against this accusation? How, then, is the casket lottery *not* a "lottery" in the usual sense?

4. "All that glisters is not gold." (line 65)

   Write a short fable to illustrate the truth of this moral. You might want to adopt the style of Aesop by using animal characters, or you might use a more realistic and contemporary style. Illustrate your fable with original drawings, digital photos, or clip art.

For the next scene . . .

Why do people sometimes laugh at the misfortune of others? How do comedians take advantage of this human tendency to make an audience laugh? When does this sense of humour cross the line into "bad taste"? When have you felt uncomfortable or uneasy with this kind of humour?

Act 2, Scene 8

In this scene . . .

Back in Venice, Salerio and Solanio discuss the whereabouts of Lorenzo. Shylock, as might be expected, has assumed that Bassanio conspired with Lorenzo and Jessica to help them escape to Belmont. However, Antonio has sworn that the lovers did not sail with Bassanio. Solanio entertains Salerio with an impersonation of the outraged Shylock. Salerio then describes the tearful parting of Antonio and Bassanio the previous evening, and expresses the fear that Antonio may well suffer the consequences of Shylock's fury against his daughter.

4   *rais'd:* roused (from sleep)

7   *given to understand:* told

10   *certified:* assured, convinced

12   *passion:* emotional outburst

13   *outrageous:* excessive, uncontrolled

25   *look he keep his day:* be careful to make his repayment on the appointed day

26   *well remember'd:* a good point to keep in mind

27   *reason'd:* talked

29   *miscarried:* perished, was lost

30   *richly fraught:* carrying rich cargo

Scene 8

Venice. A street.

Enter Salerio and Solanio.

Salerio: Why, man, I saw Bassanio under sail,
　With him is Gratiano gone along;
　And in their ship I am sure Lorenzo is not.
Solanio: The villain Jew with outcries rais'd the duke,
　Who went with him to search Bassanio's ship. 　　　　5
Salerio: He came too late, the ship was under sail,
　But there the duke was given to understand
　That in a gondola were seen together
　Lorenzo and his amorous Jessica.
　Besides, Antonio certified the duke 　　　　　　　10
　They were not with Bassanio in his ship.
Solanio: I never heard a passion so confus'd,
　So strange, outrageous, and so variable,
　As the dog Jew did utter in the streets:
　'My daughter! O my ducats! O my daughter! 　　　15
　Fled with a Christian! O my Christian ducats!
　Justice! the law! my ducats, and my daughter!
　A sealed bag, two sealed bags of ducats,
　Of double ducats, stol'n from me by my daughter!
　And jewels! two stones, two rich and precious stones, 　20
　Stol'n by my daughter! Justice! find the girl!
　She hath the stones upon her, and the ducats.'
Salerio: Why, all the boys in Venice follow him,
　Crying his stones, his daughter, and his ducats.
Solanio: Let good Antonio look he keep his day, 　　25
　Or he shall pay for this.
Salerio: 　　　　　　　　Marry, well remember'd.
　I reason'd with a Frenchman yesterday,
　Who told me, in the narrow seas that part
　The French and English, there miscarried
　A vessel of our country richly fraught. 　　　　　30

35   *treads:* walks

39   *Slubber not business:* do not rush and be careless about
        your business
40   *the very riping of the time:* until the right moment

44   *ostents:* expressions, demonstrations
45   *As shall . . . there:* as will create a good impression of you
        in Belmont

48   *wondrous sensible:* amazingly tender

50   *he only loves . . . for him:* Antonio cares about the world
        only because of his close friendship with Bassanio.
52   *quicken:* enliven, make more active, cheerful, give life to; *his
        embraced heaviness:* the seriousness that he has adopted

I thought upon Antonio when he told me,
And wish'd in silence that it were not his.
Solanio: You were best to tell Antonio what you hear;
    Yet do not suddenly, for it may grieve him.
Salerio: A kinder gentleman treads not the earth.   35
    I saw Bassanio and Antonio part:
    Bassanio told him he would make some speed
    Of his return: he answer'd, 'Do not so;
    Slubber not business for my sake, Bassanio,
    But stay the very riping of the time;   40
    And for the Jew's bond which he hath of me,
    Let it not enter in your mind of love:
    Be merry, and employ your chiefest thoughts
    To courtship and such fair ostents of love
    As shall conveniently become you there.'   45
    And even there, his eye being big with tears,
    Turning his face, he put his hand behind him,
    And with affection wondrous sensible
    He wrung Bassanio's hand; and so they parted.
Solanio: I think he only loves the world for him.   50
    I pray thee, let us go and find him out,
    And quicken his embraced heaviness
    With some delight or other.
Salerio: Do we so.

                                   [Exeunt]

Act 2, Scene 8: Activities

1. How do you respond to Solanio's description of Shylock's reactions to the elopement (lines 12–22)? Record your response in your journal, taking the following questions into consideration: How does the impersonation increase or lessen your sympathy for Shylock? How does it affect your attitude toward Solanio and his friends? How comfortable do you feel about sharing Solanio's humour?

   Imagine that there was another character—a friend of Shylock's—observing his discovery of the elopement. How would that person's version of the events differ from Solanio's? Write a modern version of the speech that he would deliver in place of Solanio's, mimicking the metre of the original.

2. Do you agree with Solanio that Shylock will try to punish Antonio for Jessica's elopement? Why would he do so? Compose the entry Shylock might write in his diary upon returning from his humiliating parade through the streets. What connections does he make between the loss of his daughter and his agreement with Antonio?

   Be sure to include all the events, from Shylock's leaving for dinner with Bassanio to his return home for the night.

3. The fact that Shylock knows his daughter has eloped with Lorenzo suggests that Jessica might have left him a letter. Compose the letter that you think Jessica would have left.

4. *Melodrama* is a form of theatre in which emotional scenes and speeches are dramatized in a heightened or exaggerated style. Television soap operas, particularly their "tear-jerking" scenes, provide the best contemporary examples. Salerio's description of Bassanio and Antonio at the end of this scene might be considered melodramatic.

   With a partner, improvise and script a new dialogue between Antonio and Bassanio, avoiding melodrama but capturing the spirit of their friendship. Be prepared to present your scripts to the class.

For the next scene . . .

Have you ever tried to judge your own work? Why is it
difficult? Would you ever try to judge your own merit as
a person? What is the chief danger in attempting this?

Act 2, Scene 9

In this scene . . .

In Belmont, Portia has a new suitor, the Prince of Arragon. Portia reminds him that, if he chooses to try the casket lottery and fails, he will have to abide by three promises. Arragon surveys the inscriptions on the caskets. Scornful of popular taste and driven by his overblown sense of self-worth, Arragon makes his choice. Just as he is reading the scroll he finds inside the casket, news arrives that Bassanio has reached Belmont.

2   *ta'en:* taken

3   *election:* selection, choice

6   *nuptial rites be solemniz'd:* marriage ceremony be performed

9   *enjoin'd:* committed, bound

10   *unfold:* reveal

11-12   *fail Of the right casket:* fail to choose correctly

16   *injunctions:* commands, restrictions

21   *You:* Arragon addresses the leaden casket directly; *ere:*
         before

25   *multitude:* the masses, common or ordinary people; *show:*
         outward appearance

26   *fond:* foolish

27   *pries not:* does not pry (look) into; *like the martlet:* The mart-
         let is a bird that builds its nest on the outward walls of build-
         ings, thus exposing its nest to the dangers of unpredictable
         weather.

Scene 9

Belmont. A room in Portia's house.

Enter Nerissa, with a Servant.

Nerissa: Quick, quick, I pray thee; draw the curtain straight:
    The Prince of Arragon hath ta'en his oath,
    And comes to his election presently.
                     [*Curtains drawn to reveal caskets*]
    [*Enter the Prince of Arragon, Portia, and Servants*]
Portia: Behold, there stand the caskets, noble prince:
    If you choose that wherein I am contain'd,   5
    Straight shall our nuptial rites be solemniz'd;
    But if you fail, without more speech, my lord,
    You must be gone from hence immediately.
Arragon: I am enjoin'd by oath to observe three things:
    First, never to unfold to any one   10
    Which casket 'twas I chose; next, if I fail
    Of the right casket, never in my life
    To woo a maid in way of marriage; lastly,
    If I do fail in fortune of my choice,
    Immediately to leave you and be gone.   15
Portia: To these injunctions every one doth swear
    That comes to hazard for my worthless self.
Arragon: And so have I address'd me. Fortune now
    To my heart's hope! Gold, silver, and base lead.
    'Who chooseth me must give and hazard all he hath.'   20
    You shall look fairer, ere I give or hazard.
    What says the golden chest? ha! let me see:
    'Who chooseth me shall gain what many men desire'.
    What many men desire! that 'many' may be meant
    By the fool multitude, that choose by show,   25
    Not learning more than the fond eye doth teach,
    Which pries not to th' interior, but, like the martlet,
    Builds in the weather on the outward wall,
    Even in the force and road of casualty.

31	*jump with:* go along with
32	*rank me with:* join (the ranks of); *barbarous:* coarse, unrefined

37	*cozen:* cheat
37-38	*be honourable . . . merit:* gain reputation (*honour*) without deserving it
40	*estates, degrees, and offices:* possessions, social rank, and positions
41	*deriv'd:* gained; *clear:* pure, bright, unsullied
42	*purchas'd:* won
43	*cover:* wear a hat. In Shakespearean times, the lower classes were expected to bare their heads in the presence of the aristocracy.
45	*glean'd:* culled, picked out
45-48	In this passage, Arragon implies that many of the nobility deserve to be peasants. Conversely, some peasants deserve to be aristocrats.
46	*seed of honour:* children of the nobility
47	*chaff and ruin of the times:* the poorest and lowest of people
50	*desert:* that I deserve
53	*portrait:* depiction (not necessarily a painting)
54	*schedule:* scroll

60	*To offend . . . offices:* those who commit an offence may not be their own judges

62	*The fire . . . tried this:* Silver is refined (*tried*) in a furnace seven times to guarantee its purity.
63-64	*Seven times . . . choose amiss:* A person's judgment must be as refined as pure silver to avoid choosing wrongly (*amiss*).

I will not choose what many men desire,   30
Because I will not jump with common spirits
And rank me with the barbarous multitudes.
Why, then to thee, thou silver treasure-house;
Tell me once more what title thou dost bear:
'Who chooseth me shall get as much as he deserves'.   35
And well said too; for who shall go about
To cozen fortune, and be honourable
Without the stamp of merit? Let none presume
To wear an undeserved dignity.
O that estates, degrees, and offices   40
Were not deriv'd corruptly, and that clear honour
Where purchas'd by the merit of the wearer.
How many then should cover that stand bare!
How many be commanded that command!
How much low peasantry would then be glean'd   45
From the true seed of honour! and how much honour
Pick'd from the chaff and ruin of the times
To be new varnish'd! Well, but to my choice:
'Who chooseth me shall get as much as he deserves'.
I will assume desert. Give me a key for this,   50
And instantly unlock my fortunes here.
                    [He opens the silver casket]
Portia: Too long a pause for that which you find there.
Arragon: What's here? the portrait of a blinking idiot,
    Presenting me a schedule! I will read it.
    How much unlike art thou to Portia!   55
    How much unlike my hopes and my deservings!
    'Who chooseth me shall have as much as he deserves'.
    Did I deserve no more than a fool's head?
    Is that my prize? are my deserts no better?
Portia: To offend, and judge, are distinct offices,   60
    And of opposed natures.
Arragon: What is here?

    The fire seven times tried this:
    Seven times tried that judgment is
    That did never choose amiss
    Some there be that shadows kiss: 65
    Such have but a shadow's bliss.

67 *iwis:* indeed, certainly

68 *Silver'd o'er:* covered with silver (so that the foolishness is hidden). The scroll makes reference to old men whose silver hair makes them appear wise.

69 *Take what wife you will to bed:* (How does this advice ignore the "rules" or the casket lottery?)

71 *sped:* finished

78 *sing'd:* burned

79 *deliberate fools:* fools who deliberate (reason) too much

81 *no heresy:* true, not a false belief

82 *"Hanging and wiving goes by destiny":* (Put Nerissa's proverb into your own words.)

85 *alighted:* dismounted (from his horse)

86 *before:* in advance, ahead of

87 *signify:* announce

88 *sensible regreets:* tangible greetings (in the form of gifts)

89 *To wit:* that is to say; *commends:* compliments; *breath:* words, speech

90 *Yet:* until now

91 *likely:* fitting

93 *costly:* rich, bountiful

94 *fore-spurrer:* messenger, herald

96 *anon:* soon; *kin:* relation

97 *high-day:* high-flown, extravagant

99 *post:* messenger; *mannerly:* with such courtesy

100 *lord Love:* Cupid, the young god of love

> *There be fools alive, iwis,*
> *Silver'd o'er; and so was this.*
> *Take what wife you will to bed,*
> *I will ever be your head.* 70
> *So be gone: you are sped.*

Still more fool I shall appear
By the time I linger here:
With one fool's head I came to woo,
But I go away with two. 75
Sweet, adieu. I'll keep my oath,
Patiently to bear my wrath.
        [*Exit Arragon with his Servants*]
Portia: Thus hath the candle sing'd the moth.
  O these deliberate fools! when they do choose,
  They have the wisdom by their wit to lose. 80
Nerissa: The ancient saying is no heresy:
  'Hanging and wiving goes by destiny.'
Portia: Come, draw the curtain, Nerissa.
  [*Enter a Servant*]
Servant: Where is my lady?
Portia: Here; what would my lord?
Servant: Madam, there is alighted at your gate 85
  A young Venetian, one that comes before
  To signify th' approaching of his lord;
  From whom he bringeth sensible regreets,
  To wit, besides commends and courteous breath,
  Gifts of rich value. Yet I have not seen 90
  So likely an ambassador of love.
  A day in April never came so sweet
  To show how costly summer was at hand,
  As this fore-spurrer comes before his lord.
Portia: No more, I pray thee: I am half afeard 95
  Thou wilt say anon he is some kin to thee,
  Thou spend'st such high-day wit in praising him.
  Come, come, Nerissa; for I long to see
  Quick Cupid's post that comes so mannerly.
Nerissa: Bassanio, lord Love, if thy will it be!   [*Exeunt*] 100

Act 2, Scene 9: Activities

1. In pairs or small groups, discuss whether Arragon's reasoning in this scene is different from that of Morocco in Act 2, Scene 7. Given Portia's father's intention that the lottery be a test of character, which of the two princes proves more worthy? Why?

2. With a partner, improvise and script a dialogue between Morocco and Arragon in which each defends his choice of casket to the other. Share your dialogue with other pairs.

3. As a class, make a list of possible reasons why Portia's father insisted that potential suitors never seek another bride. Discuss whether you think this is a fair condition for playing the "lottery."

4. You now know which casket contains the portrait of Portia. From what you have learned about Bassanio, do you think he will choose correctly? Why or why not? Discuss this question in a small group, using the list of Bassanio's characteristics that you began to compile after the first scene of the play.

5. Imagine that you are Shakespeare. The members of your acting troupe, the King's Men, have argued that this scene should be eliminated because the audience is already certain from Morocco's choice that Portia's portrait is in the leaden casket.

   Prepare and deliver to the class a speech justifying including this scene. Your speech should select and develop at least one of the scene's many dramatic, thematic, or comedic possibilities.

For the next scene . . .

"Revenge is sweet!" Recall a situation in which you seriously contemplated taking revenge on someone. Why did you want revenge? How did you plan to seek revenge? What finally determined your decision to put your plan into action or to abandon it?

Act 3, Scene 1

In this scene . . .

The action of the play returns to Venice where the bond between Antonio and Shylock is almost due. Salerio has heard bad news about one of Antonio's ships, but he is quick to realize that Shylock's determination to take revenge for Jessica's elopement is a far greater threat to his friend. When Shylock enters, Salerio asks him outright what possible use a pound of human flesh could be. Shylock's famous answer contains not only an eloquent defence of his own humanity, but also a clear indication that nothing will distract him from full revenge on his enemies. Tubal enters with upsetting news of the way Jessica has been wasting the money and jewels she stole. He soothes Shylock with a prediction of Antonio's bankruptcy.

2   *yet it lives:* there is a persistent rumour; *unchecked:* undenied

3   *lading:* cargo; *the narrow seas:* the English Channel (between England and France)

4   *the Goodwins:* the Goodwin Sands, a sandbar in the middle of the English Channel

5   *flat:* sandbar

6   *my gossip Report:* the old woman who is my informer (Report or Rumour is personified here)

8   *I would:* I wish; *that:* her report

9   *knapped:* chewed, nibbled; *ginger:* Ginger was commonly associated with old people in Elizabethan times. It may have been a digestive aid.

11   *prolixity:* long-windedness

15   *Come, the full stop:* Come to your point!

19   *betimes:* immediately. Solanio wants to conclude Salerio's prayer with the formal *amen* (so be it) before it can be foiled by the devil; *cross:* thwart. Note the pun. Some Christians make the sign of the cross when they have finished a prayer. The devil, of course, would never bless or answer a prayer, but would frustrate (*cross*) its intentions.

25   *withal:* with

27   *fledge:* fledged, ready to fly (with new feathers on its young wings); *complexion:* nature, disposition

28   *dam:* mother

30   *the devil:* Salerio means Shylock. Note his earlier comparison in line 20.

Act 3, Scene 1

Venice. A street.

Enter Solanio and Salerio.

Solanio: Now, what news on the Rialto?

Salerio: Why, yet it lives there unchecked that Antonio hath
a ship of rich lading wrecked on the narrow seas—
the Goodwins, I think they call the place, a very
dangerous flat, and fatal, where the carcasses of many   5
a tall ship lie buried, as they say, if my gossip Report
be an honest woman of her word.

Solanio: I would she were as lying a gossip in that as ever
knapped ginger, or made her neighbours believe she
wept for the death of a third husband. But it is true—   10
without any slips of prolixity or crossing the plain
highway of talk—that the good Antonio, the honest
Antonio—O, that I had a tide good enough to keep his
name company!

Salerio: Come, the full stop.   15

Solanio: Ha! what say'st thou? Why, the end is, he hath
lost a ship.

Salerio: I would it might prove the end of his losses.

Solanio: Let me say 'amen' betimes, lest the devil cross my
prayer, for here he comes, in the likeness of a Jew.   20
[*Enter Shylock*]
How now, Shylock! what news among the merchants?

Shylock: You knew, none so well, none so well as you, of
my daughter's flight.

Salerio: That's certain: I, for my part, knew the tailor that
made the wings she flew withal.   25

Solanio: And Shylock, for his own part, knew the bird was
fledge; and then it is the complexion of them all to
leave the dam.

Shylock: She is damned for it.

Salerio: That's certain, if the devil may be her judge.   30

Shylock: My own flesh and blood to rebel!

32   *Out upon it:* curse it (your body); *old carrion:* old man (with a tired and decaying body); *rebels it at these years:* Do you still feel lust at your age? Solanio pretends that Shylock is referring to the rebellion of his own body against his mind and insults him by suggesting that he no longer has control over his sexual urges. Shylock clarifies his meaning in the next line.

35   *jet:* a black mineral

36   *Rhenish:* white wine from the Rhine Valley in Germany

39   *match:* bargain

41   *that was used to:* who used to; *smug:* neatly and richly dressed (How does the more modern meaning of the words also apply here?)

42   *mart:* marketplace; *look to:* pay attention to (both "look after" and "be careful of"); *wont:* accustomed

43   *usurer:* "loan shark"

44   *for a Christian courtesy:* as a favour. Charity (love for one's fellow human being) is considered the greatest of Christian virtues.

48   *To bait fish withal:* to use as bait for fishing

50   *hindered me:* prevented me (from earning a profit)

52   *bargains:* business deals; *cooled . . . heated:* (What does Shylock mean here?)

54   *dimensions:* bodily size and shape

63   *what is his humility?:* What happens to the humbleness or meekness that the New Testament commands (*Matthew* 5:39–44)? Shylock answers his own question in a single word, *Revenge!*

64   *what should his sufferance be:* How should he endure it? Shylock is prepared to disregard this Jewish virtue ("For sufferance is the badge of all our tribe," Act 1, Scene 3, line 106) as readily as the Christian disregards his humility.

66-67   *it shall go hard but . . . the instruction:* No matter what happens, I will be even more vengeful than you have taught me to be.

Solanio: Out upon it, old carrion! rebels it at these years?

Shylock: I say my daughter is my flesh and my blood.

Salerio: There is more difference between thy flesh and hers
    than between jet and ivory; more between your bloods   35
    than there is between red wine and Rhenish. But tell
    us, do you hear whether Antonio have had any loss
    at sea or no?

Shylock: There I have another bad match: a bankrupt, a
    prodigal, who dare scarce show his head on the Rialto;   40
    a beggar, that was used to come so smug upon the
    mart. Let him look to his bond! he was wont to call
    me usurer. Let him look to his bond! he was wont
    to lend money for a Christian courtesy. Let him look
    to his bond!   45

Salerio: Why, I am sure, if he forfeit thou wilt not take his
    flesh: what's that good for?

Shylock: To bait fish withal: if it will feed nothing else, it
    will feed my revenge. He hath disgraced me, and
    hindered me half a million, laughed at my losses,   50
    mocked at my gains, scorned my nation, thwarted my
    bargains, cooled my friends, heated mine enemies; and
    what's his reason? I am a Jew. Hath not a Jew eyes?
    hath not a Jew hands, organs, dimensions, senses,
    affections, passions? fed with the same food, hurt   55
    with the same weapons, subject to the same diseases,
    healed by the same means, warmed and cooled by
    the same winter and summer, as a Christian is? If you
    prick us, do we not bleed? if you tickle us, do we not
    laugh? if you poison us, do we not die? and if you   60
    wrong us, shall we not revenge? If we are like you in
    the rest, we will resemble you in that. If a Jew wrong
    a Christian, what is his humility? Revenge! If a
    Christian wrong a Jew, what should his sufferance be
    by Christian example? Why, revenge! The villainy   65
    you teach me I will execute, and it shall go hard but I
    will better the instruction.

    [*Enter a Servant*]

Servant: Gentlemen, my master Antonio is at his house,
    and desires to speak with you both.

Salerio: We have been up and down to seek him.   70

71-72   *a third cannot be matched:* these two cannot be matched by a third

78   *Frankfurt:* In medieval times, an international fair was held in Frankfurt, Germany, twice each year.

79-80   *I never felt it till now:* Shylock discounts the history of the persecution and suffering of his people in comparison with his own misery.

83   *hearsed:* laid out in her coffin

88   *but what lights o':* except what alights on, lands on

88-89   *but o' my breathing:* except the ones that I breathe

93   *cast away:* wrecked

100   *fourscore:* eighty (a score is twenty)

102   *at a sitting:* on a single occasion, at one time

104   *divers:* several

106   *break:* go broke, declare bankruptcy

[*Enter Tubal*]

Solanio: Here comes another of the tribe: a third cannot be
    matched, unless the devil himself turn Jew.

                  [*Exeunt Solanio, Salerio, and Servant*]

Shylock: How now, Tubal! what news from Genoa? Hast
    thou found my daughter?

Tubal: I often came where I did hear of her, but cannot   75
    find her.

Shylock: Why there, there, there, there! a diamond gone,
    cost me two thousand ducats in Frankfurt! The curse
    never fell upon our nation till now; I never felt it
    till now: two thousand ducats in that, and other   80
    precious, precious jewels. I would my daughter were
    dead at my foot, and the jewels in her ear! would she
    were hearsed at my foot, and the ducats in her coffin!
    No news of them—why so? and I know not what's
    spent in the search. Why thou—loss upon loss! the thief   85
    gone with so much, and so much to find the thief;
    and no satisfaction, no revenge: nor no ill luck stirring
    but what lights o' my shoulders; no sighs but o' my
    breathing; no tears but o' my shedding.

Tubal: Yes, other men have ill luck too. Antonio, as I heard   90
    in Genoa—

Shylock: What, what, what? ill luck? ill luck?

Tubal:—hath an argosy cast away, coming from Tripolis.

Shylock: I thank God! I thank God! Is it true? is it true?

Tubal: I spoke with some of the sailors that escaped the   95
    wreck.

Shylock: I thank thee, good Tubal. Good news, good news!
    ha, ha! Heard in Genoa?

Tubal: Your daughter spent in Genoa, as I heard, one night,
    fourscore ducats.   100

Shylock: Thou stick'st a dagger in me: I shall never see my
    gold again: fourscore ducats at a sitting! fourscore
    ducats!

Tubal: There came divers of Antonio's creditors in my
    company in Venice, that swear he cannot choose but   105
    break.

Shylock: I am very glad of it: I'll plague him; I'll torture
    him: I am glad of it.

109-110 *of your daughter:* from your daughter

111   *Out upon her!:* Curse her! Damn her!

112   *I had it of Leah:* It was a gift from Leah, Shylock's late wife.

115-116 *fee me an officer:* hire an officer (to arrest Antonio)

116   *bespeak him a fortnight before:* Order him to be ready two weeks before the bond falls due.

117-118 *were he out . . . I will:* If he were gone from Venice, I would be able to conduct my business unhindered and unchecked.

Tubal: One of them showed me a ring that he had of your
    daughter for a monkey. 110

Shylock: Out upon her! Thou torturest me, Tubal: it was
    my turquoise; I had it of Leah when I was a bachelor:
    I would not have given it for a wilderness of monkeys.

Tubal: But Antonio is certainly undone.

Shylock: Nay, that's true, that's very true. Go, Tubal, fee 115
    me an officer; bespeak him a fortnight before. I will
    have the heart of him, if he forfeit; for, were he out
    of Venice, I can make what merchandise I will. Go,
    Tubal, and meet me at our synagogue; go, good
    Tubal; at our synagogue, Tubal. 120

                           [Exeunt in different directions]

Act 3, Scene 1: Activities

1. Solanio's and Salerio's mockery brings Shylock to an emotional outburst in which he "justifies" revenge (lines 48–67).

    a) In a small group, read the speech aloud several times so that you can fully appreciate Shylock's words. Then, trace the logical steps in Shylock's argument.

    b) Decide what your group considers to be the strongest and the weakest points of Shylock's argument, and report your findings to the class. Do different groups have different interpretations?

    c) As a group, decide on the best placement of pauses and stresses, and on the most effective modulations of volume and pitch. Finally, agree on the body language that should accompany the words. Then, choose a representative to perform your version of the speech before the class.

2. In this scene, Tubal returns from his mission to locate Jessica in Genoa. With a partner, improvise or script the "missing" scene in which Shylock sends Tubal to Genoa to search for his missing daughter and money. As playwrights, consider these questions:

    • What is Shylock's state of mind as he issues Tubal his instructions?

    • What are his purposes and priorities in sending Tubal to Genoa?

    • What is Tubal to do, if and when he finds Jessica?

    • What is Tubal's attitude toward his assignment?

    Compare your scenes with those of other pairs. Note and discuss differences in interpretation, especially of Shylock's character.

3. This is the only scene in which Tubal appears. With a partner, discuss the purpose of his appearance. Is his character necessary? Why or why not? Share your conclusions with the rest of the class.

Rehearse and present your version of his conversation with Shylock to the class, or tape it on an audio or video recording. Consider the following questions when playing the part of Tubal:

- Is he old or young?

- Is he clever or slow?

- Is he comic or serious?

- Is he sympathetic or indifferent to Shylock's feelings?

Be sure to think about the way in which Tubal's personality and attitude may affect the audience's perception of Shylock.

4. "I would not have given it for a wilderness of monkeys." Shylock's reaction to the thoughtless sale of his precious memento of Leah (presumably his late wife) reveals that he can be tender and sentimental. Write a letter from the young Shylock to Leah that shows this aspect of his character. Establish a specific context for the letter: a time, a place, and an occasion. You might consider a letter of thanks for the ring, a first love letter, a formal proposal of marriage, or a letter from overseas. Conversely, you may wish to write as Leah to Shylock, urging him to accept your gift.

5. Return to the question from Act 2, Scene 1, Activity 5, and your diagram of the relationships among the *dramatis personae*. Update your diagram with new information.

For the next scene ...

What are the criteria by which we should judge the true value of something? How do "covers" often confuse us?

Act 3, Scene 2

In this scene . . .

In Belmont, Portia and Bassanio have fallen in love, and all thoughts of time and obligation have passed from Bassanio's mind. Bassanio is eager, however, to have Portia as his wife and is anxious to make his casket choice. Portia begs him to wait a few days longer, but Bassanio cannot bear the torture of further delay. After contemplating the difference between appearance and reality, he chooses the lead casket and wins Portia as his wife. Gratiano adds to the mood of celebration with news of his own marriage plans, and an exchange of rings and promises brings the scene to a climax of happiness and joy.

However, the mood alters after Lorenzo and Jessica arrive unexpectedly with Salerio, who has brought a letter for Bassanio from Venice. Antonio has written to announce that all of his ships have been lost. Three months have passed since his bond with Shylock was signed and he is now completely within Shylock's power.

1   *tarry:* wait

2   *hazard:* take a risk

3   *forbear:* hold back

5   *I would not:* I do not want to

6   *Hate counsels . . . quality:* Hatred does not give this kind of advice.

10   *venture:* take a risk

11   *I am forsworn:* I would be breaking my promise (for her promise, see Act 1, Scene 2, lines 102–104)

12   *So:* in this situation (that is, forsworn); *miss:* lose

14   *Beshrew:* shame on

15   *o'erlook'd:* cast a spell upon, bewitched

20   *Prove it so:* if it should prove so, if it turns out this way

22   *peise:* slow down

23   *eke it . . . in length:* make it last

24   *To stay you from election:* to delay you from making your choice

25   *rack:* an instrument of torture that stretched the victim's body over a wooden frame. The rack was commonly used to force confessions from suspected traitors and heretics.

29   *fear th' enjoying of my love:* be afraid that I shall never have the one I love

Scene 2

Belmont. A room in Portia's house.
Enter Bassanio, Portia, Gratiano,
Nerissa, and Servants.

Portia: I pray you, tarry, pause a day or two
  Before you hazard; for, in choosing wrong,
  I lose your company: therefore, forbear awhile.
  There's something tells me (but it is not love)
  I would not lose you; and you know yourself,   5
  Hate counsels not in such a quality.
  But lest you should not understand me well—
  And yet a maiden hath no tongue but thought—
  I would detain you here some month or two
  Before you venture for me. I could teach you   10
  How to choose right, but then I am forsworn;
  So will I never be: so may you miss me—
  But if you do, you'll make me wish a sin,
  That I had been forsworn. Beshrew your eyes,
  They have o'erlook'd me and divided me: 15
  One half of me is yours, the other half yours—
  Mine own, I would say; but if mine, then yours,
  And so all yours. O these naughty times
  Put bars between the owners and their rights;
  And so, though yours, not yours. Prove it so,   20
  Let fortune go to hell for it, not I.
  I speak too long; but 'tis to peise the time,
  To eke it and to draw it out in length,
  To stay you from election.
Bassanio: Let me choose;
  For as I am, I live upon the rack.   25
Portia: Upon the rack, Bassanio! then confess
  What treason there is mingled with your love.
Bassanio: None but that ugly treason of mistrust,
  Which makes me fear th' enjoying of my love:

30-31	*There may as well . . . my love:* There is as little friendship (*amity*) between snow and fire as there is between treason and my love.
33	*enforced:* forced (by the pain of the torture)
36	*Had been . . . confession:* is all I have to confess
38	*deliverance:* release
42	*aloof:* aside, to the side
44	*a swan-like end:* Swans do not sing. However, the Elizabethans believed that a swan did sing a beautiful lament immediately before its death.
46	*May stand more proper:* may be complete (Decipher the full meaning of Portia's metaphor.)
49	*flourish:* fanfare
51	*dulcet:* sweet
54	*presence:* dignity, nobility
55	*Alcides:* Hercules, who was the son of Alcaeus. Hercules rescued the Trojan princess Hesione, who had been offered by her father as a sacrifice to the sea-monster that was threatening to destroy Troy.
58	*Dardanian:* Trojan (descended from Dardanus, the legendary founder of Troy)
59	*bleared visages:* tear-stained faces
60	*issue:* outcome
61	*Live thou:* if you live
62	*fray:* fight
63	*fancy:* infatuation, shallow love, love based upon physical attraction
65	*begot:* begun

There may as well be amity and life   30
   'Tween snow and fire, as treason and my love.
Portia: Ay, but I fear you speak upon the rack,
   Where men enforced do speak anything.
Bassanio: Promise me life, and I'll confess the truth.
Portia: Well, then, confess, and live.   35
Bassanio: 'Confess and love'
   Had been the very sum of my confession:
   O happy torment, when my torturer
   Doth teach me answers for deliverance!
   But let me to my fortune and the caskets.
Portia: Away then! I am lock'd in one of them: 40
   If you do love me, you will find me out.
   Nerissa and the rest, stand all aloof.
   Let music sound while he doth make his choice;
   Then, if he lose, he makes a swan-like end,
   Fading in music: that the comparison   45
   May stand more proper, my eye shall be the stream
   And watery death-bed for him. He may win;
   And what is music then? then music is
   Even as the flourish when true subjects bow
   To a new-crowned monarch: such it is   50
   As are those dulcet sounds in break of day
   That creep into the dreaming bridegroom's ear,
   And summon him to marriage. Now he goes,
   With no less presence, but with much more love,
   Than young Alcides, when he did redeem   55
   The virgin tribute paid by howling Troy
   To the sea-monster: I stand for sacrifice;
   The rest aloof are the Dardanian wives,
   With bleared visages come forth to view
   The issue of th' exploit. Go, Hercules!   60
   Live thou, I live: with much, much more dismay
   I view the fight than thou that mak'st the fray.
   [A Song whilst Bassanio comments on the caskets to himself.]

     Tell me where is fancy bred,
     Or in the heart or in the head?
     How begot, how nourished?   65
       Reply, reply.

67   *engend'red:* born, begotten

70   *knell:* funeral bell

73   *least themselves:* not in the least what they appear to be

74   *The world:* people; *still:* continually, forever; *ornament:* outward appearance

75-77   *In law . . . show of evil:* In a court, a legal argument, however faulty and dishonest, may sound convincing when it is disguised by a brilliant speaker.

78   *damned error:* false belief; *sober brow:* seemingly honest and educated person   ·

79   *text:* a passage from the Bible (Compare this with Antonio's remark in Act 1, Scene 3, line 94.)

81-82   *There is no vice . . . outward parts:* All vices may be disguised by an outward show of virtue.

85   *beards:* Beards were considered to be a sign of manliness and courage. *Mars:* the classical god of war

86   *livers white as milk:* The liver of a brave person would be red with blood (compare with Morocco's boast in Act 2, Scene 1, line 7). The liver of a coward would be white.

87   *valour's excrement:* the outward show (beards) of courage

88   *To render them redoubted:* to make them look frightening

88-89   *Look on beauty . . . weight:* In Elizabethan times, cosmetics were sold by weight.

91   *lightest:* both *lightest* in colour (therefore, fairest, most beautiful) and *lightest* in morality (least pure, least innocent)

92-95   *So are those . . . second head:* In Elizabethan times, wigs were made with hair cut from corpses.

97   *guiled:* full of guile or deceit

99   *Indian beauty:* Dark beauty would have been a contradiction in terms for Shakespeare's audience.

102   *Hard food for Midas:* According to Greek legend, King Midas of Phrygia in Asia Minor was so greedy that he wished that all he touched might become gold. Once his wish came true, he almost starved to death.

103   *common drudge:* lowly servant (*common* because silver passes from hand to hand as coins)

104   *meagre:* poor, undecorated

105   *aught:* anything

It is engend'red in the eyes,
With gazing fed; and fancy dies
In the cradle where it lies.
   Let us all ring fancy's knell: 70
   I'll begin it—Ding, dong, bell.
   Ding, dong, bell.

Bassanio: So may the outward shows be least themselves:
   The world is still deceiv'd with ornament.
   In law, what plea so tainted and corrupt   75
   But, being season'd with a gracious voice,
   Obscures the show of evil? In religion,
   What damned error, but some sober brow
   Will bless it and approve it with a text,
   Hiding the grossness with fair ornament?   80
   There is no vice so simple but assumes
   Some mark of virtue on his outward parts.
   How many cowards, whose hearts are all as false
   As stairs of sand, wear yet upon their chins
   The beards of Hercules and frowning Mars,   85
   Who, inward search'd, have livers white as milk;
   And these assume but valour's excrement
   To render them redoubted. Look on beauty,
   And you shall see 'tis purchas'd by the weight;
   Which therein works a miracle in nature,   90
   Making them lightest that wear most of it:
   So are those crisped snaky golden locks
   Which make such wanton gambols with the wind,
   Upon supposed fairness, often known
   To be the dowry of a second head,   95
   The skull that bred them in the sepulchre.
   Thus ornament is but the guiled shore
   To a more dangerous sea, the beauteous scarf
   Veiling an Indian beauty; in a word,
   The seeming truth which cunning times put on   100
   To entrap the wisest. Therefore, thou gaudy gold,
   Hard food for Midas, I will none of thee;
   Nor none of thee, thou pale and common drudge
   'Tween man and man: but thou, thou meagre lead,
   Which rather threaten'st than dost promise aught,   105

107	*consequence:* result, outcome
108	*fleet to:* vanish into
109	*As:* such as; *rash-embrac'd:* too quickly accepted
110	*green-eyed jealousy:* Compare with the expression *green with envy.*
111	*allay:* restrain
112	*measure:* moderation; *scant:* restrain
114	*surfeit:* suffer from having too much
115	*counterfeit:* likeness, portrait
115-116	*What demi-god . . . creation?:* What artist was so divine that he was able to paint a picture so remarkably life-like?
116	*Move these eyes?:* Do these eyes move?
117	*riding . . . mine:* controlled by my own gazing
118	*sever'd:* parted
119-120	*so sweet a bar . . . sweet friends:* It is appropriate that such sweet breath should part such sweet lips.
120-123	*Here in her hairs . . . gnats in cobwebs:* Bassanio compares Portia's hair to a spider's web. (Do you find this metaphor either appropriate or flattering?)
125	*it:* the one eye that he has already painted
126	*unfurnish'd:* unpartnered (by a second eye)
126-129	*yet look . . . substance:* Just as my praise cannot adequately describe the beauty of this portrait, so the portrait does not capture the beauty of Portia herself.
130	*continent:* container
140	*by note:* according to the instructions (found in lines 137–138)
141	*contending in a prize:* competing in a contest (fencing, wrestling, archery, or some other sport)

Thy paleness moves me more than eloquence,
And here choose I: joy be the consequence!
Portia: [*Aside*] How all the other passions fleet to air,
As doubtful thoughts, and rash-embrac'd despair,
And shuddering fear, and green-eyed jealousy.   110
O love be moderate, allay thy ecstasy,
In measure rain thy joy, scant this excess,
I feel too much thy blessing; make it less,
For fear I surfeit!
Bassanio: What find I here?
                              [*He opens the leaden casket*]
Fair Portia's counterfeit! What demi-god   115
Hath come so near creation? Move these eyes?
Or whether, riding on the balls of mine,
Seem they in motion? Here are sever'd lips,
Parted with sugar breath; so sweet a bar
Should sunder such sweet friends. Here in her hairs   120
The painter plays the spider, and hath woven
A golden mesh t'entrap the hearts of men
Faster than gnats in cobwebs: but her eyes!
How could he see to do them? having made one,
Methinks it should have power to steal both his   125
And leave itself unfurnish'd: yet look how far
The substance of my praise doth wrong this shadow
In underprizing it, so far this shadow
Doth limp behind the substance. Here's the scroll,
The continent and summary of my fortune.   130

> *You that choose not by the view,*
> *Chance as fair, and choose as true!*
> *Since this fortune falls to you,*
> *Be content and seek no new.*
> *If you be well pleas'd with this*   135
> *And hold your fortune for your bliss,*
> *Turn you where your lady is*
> *And claim her with a loving kiss.*

A gentle scroll. Fair lady, by your leave;
                              [*Kissing her*]
I come by note, to give and to receive.   140
Like one of two contending in a prize,

143   *universal shout:* shouts of support from everyone
144   *in a doubt:* uncertainly, unsurely
145   *his or no:* for him or not

148   *ratified:* formally guaranteed (that is, with the kiss promised
         by the scroll)

153   *trebled:* tripled

155   *That only to:* only so that I may; *account:* estimation, opinion
156   *livings:* material possessions
157   *Exceed account:* be worth more than you can estimate
158   *to term in gross:* to put it bluntly or to state in full
159   *unpractis'd:* inexperienced
160   *Happy:* fortunate, lucky (as well as *happy* in the modern
         sense)
162   *is not bred so dull:* was not born so stupid

167   *but now:* just a moment ago

173   *presage the ruin:* signify or represent the end
174   *vantage to exclaim on you:* opportunity to reproach you
175   *bereft me:* taken from me
176   *Only my blood . . . veins:* Only my blushing tells you what I
         feel.
177-183 *And there is . . . not express'd:* Bassanio compares himself
         to a crowd that is overcome with joy as it responds to a rous-
         ing speech by its beloved prince.

That thinks he hath done well in people's eyes,
Hearing applause and universal shout,
Giddy in spirit, still gazing in a doubt
Whether those peals of praise be his or no;   145
So, thrice-fair lady, stand I, even so,
As doubtful whether what I see be true,
Until confirm'd, sign'd, ratified by you.
Portia: You see me, Lord Bassanio, where I stand,
Such as I am: though for myself alone   150
I would not be ambitious in my wish,
To wish myself much better; yet, for you,
I would be trebled twenty times myself;
A thousand times more fair, ten thousand times
    more rich;
That only to stand high in your account,   155
I might in virtues, beauties, livings, friends,
Exceed account: but the full sum of me
Is sum of something, which, to term in gross,
Is an unlesson'd girl, unschool'd, unpractis'd;
Happy in this, she is not yet so old   160
But she may learn; happier than this,
She is not bred so dull but she can learn;
Happiest of all, is that her gentle spirit
Commits itself to yours to be directed
As from her lord, her governor, her king.   165
Myself and what is mine, to you and yours
Is now converted: but now I was the lord
Of this fair mansion, master of my servants,
Queen o'er myself; and even now, but now,
This house, these servants, and this same myself   170
Are yours, my lord's. I give them with this ring;
Which when you part from, lose, or give away,
Let it presage the ruin of your love,
And be my vantage to exclaim on you.
Bassanio: Madam, you have bereft me of all words,   175
Only my blood speaks to you in my veins;
And there is such confusion in my powers,
As, after some oration fairly spoke
By a beloved prince, there doth appear
Among the buzzing pleased multitude;   180

187   *prosper:* come true

192   *your honours:* form of address to show respect for superiors; *solemnize:* make legal (in a marriage ceremony)

193   *bargain:* contract

195   *so:* provided that

199-200 *for intermission . . . than you:* I haven't been wasting my time any more than you have been.

201   *stood:* depended

203   *until I sweat again:* so hard that I began to sweat

204   *swearing:* making promises and oaths of love; *roof:* the roof (top) of his mouth

213   *play with them:* place bets with them

214   *stake down:* put our money on the table now. In the following line, Gratiano responds with a bawdy pun.

216   *infidel:* non-Christian, in this case, Jessica

Where every something, being blent together,
Turns to a wild of nothing, save of joy,
Express'd, and not express'd. But when this ring
Parts from this finger, then parts life from hence:
O then be bold to say Bassanio's dead.   185
Nerissa: My lord and lady, it is now our time,
That have stood by and seen our wishes prosper,
To cry, good joy. Good joy, my lord and lady!
Gratiano: My Lord Bassanio, and my gentle lady,
I wish you all the joy that you can wish;   190
For I am sure you can wish none from me.
And when your honours mean to solemnize
The bargain of your faith, I do beseech you,
Even at that time I may be married too.
Bassanio: With all my heart, so thou canst get a wife.   195
Gratiano: I thank your lordship, you have got me one.
My eyes, my lord, can look as swift as yours:
You saw the mistress, I beheld the maid;
You lov'd, I lov'd: for intermission
No more pertains to me, my lord, than you.   200
Your fortune stood upon the caskets there,
And so did mine too, as the matter falls;
For wooing here until I sweat again,
And swearing till my very roof was dry
With oaths of love, at last (if promise last)   205
I got a promise of this fair one here
To have her love, provided that your fortune
Achiev'd her mistress.
Portia: Is this true, Nerissa?
Nerissa: Madam, it is, so you stand pleas'd withal.
Bassanio: And do you, Gratiano, mean good faith?   210
Gratiano: Yes, faith, my lord.
Bassanio: Our feast shall be much honour'd in your marriage.
Gratiano: We'll play with them the first boy for a thousand
ducats.
Nerissa: What, and stake down?
Gratiano: No, we shall ne'er win at that sport and stake   215
down!
But who comes here? Lorenzo and his infidel!
What! and my old Venetian friend, Salerio?

219-220 *If that the youth . . . welcome:* if I have the right to welcome you, considering that my authority here is so recent

221   *very:* true

230   *Commends him:* sends his greetings; *Ere I ope:* before I open

234   *estate:* both "state of mind" and "financial situation"

235   *yond stranger:* the stranger over there

237   *royal:* both "worthy" and "wealthy"

239   *We are the Jasons:* (See Bassanio's earlier allusion to the golden fleece in Act 1, Scene 1, line 170.)

241   *shrewd:* hurtful

244   *constitution:* temperament (as revealed by the changing colour of Bassanio's complexion)

245   *constant:* even-tempered

246   *With leave:* excuse me

250   *blotted:* stained (with ink)

[*Enter Lorenzo, Jessica, and Salerio*]

Bassanio: Lorenzo, and Salerio, welcome hither,
    If that the youth of my new interest here
    Have power to bid you welcome. By your leave,   220
    I bid my very friends and countrymen,
    Sweet Portia, welcome.
Portia: So do I, my lord:
    They are entirely welcome.
Lorenzo: I thank your honour. For my part, my lord,
    My purpose was not to have seen you here,   225
    But meeting with Salerio by the way,
    He did entreat me, past all saying nay,
    To come with him along.
Salerio: I did, my lord,
    And I have reason for it. Signior Antonio
    Commends him to you.   [*Gives Bassanio a letter*] 230
Bassanio: Ere I ope his letter,
    I pray you, tell me how my good friend doth.
Salerio: Not sick, my lord, unless it be in mind;
    Nor well, unless in mind: his letter there
    Will show you his estate.
                      [*Bassanio opens the letter*]
Gratiano: Nerissa, cheer yond stranger; bid her welcome. 235
    Your hand, Salerio. What's the news from Venice?
    How doth that royal merchant, good Antonio?
    I know he will be glad of our success;
    We are the Jasons, we have won the fleece.
Salerio: I would you had won the fleece that he hath lost. 240
Portia: There are some shrewd contents in yond same
      paper,
    That steals the colour from Bassanio's cheek:
    Some dear friend dead, else nothing in the world
    Could turn so much the constitution
    Of any constant man. What, worse and worse!   245
    With leave, Bassanio; I am half yourself,
    And I must freely have the half of anything
    That this same paper brings you.
Bassanio: O sweet Portia!
    Here are a few of the unpleasant'st words
    That ever blotted paper. Gentle lady   250

251   *impart:* confess

255   *Rating:* valuing
256   *braggart:* boaster
257   *state:* estate, fortune

259   *engag'd:* committed, bound, indebted
260   *mere:* absolute
261   *To feed my means:* to supply myself with money

265   *hit:* success

271   *present money:* ready cash; *discharge:* pay off his debt to
272   *He:* Shylock
274   *keen:* both "eager" and "cruel"; *confound:* destroy, ruin
275   *plies:* begs, urges
276   *impeach the freedom of the state:* cast doubt upon the reputation of Venice as a city of justice and equality
278   *magnificoes:* Venetian senators and noblemen
279   *port:* power, authority, social rank; *persuaded with him:* tried to persuade him
280   *envious plea:* malicious demand
281   *forfeiture:* penalty

287   *deny not:* do not prevent him

When I did first impart my love to you,
I freely told you all the wealth I had
Ran in my veins—I was a gentleman—
And then I told you true; and yet, dear lady,
Rating myself at nothing, you shall see   255
How much I was a braggart. When I told you
My state was nothing, I should then have told you
That I was worse than nothing; for, indeed,
I have engag'd myself to a dear friend,
Engag'd my friend to his mere enemy   260
To feed my means. Here is a letter, lady;
The paper as the body of my friend,
And every word in it a gaping wound,
Issuing life-blood. But is it true, Salerio?
Hath all his ventures fail'd? What, not one hit?   265
From Tripolis, from Mexico, and England,
From Lisbon, Barbary, and India?
And not one vessel 'scape the dreadful touch
Of merchant-marring rocks?
Salerio: Not one, my lord.
    Besides, it should appear, that if he had   270
    The present money to discharge the Jew,
    He would not take it. Never did I know
    A creature, that did bear the shape of man,
    So keen and greedy to confound a man.
    He plies the duke at morning and at night,   275
    And doth impeach the freedom of the state,
    If they deny him justice: twenty merchants,
    The duke himself, and the magnificoes
    Of greatest port, have all persuaded with him;
    But none can drive him from the envious plea   280
    Of forfeiture, of justice, and his bond.
Jessica: When I was with him, I have heard him swear
    To Tubal and to Chus, his countrymen,
    That he would rather have Antonio's flesh
    Than twenty times the value of the sum   285
    That he did owe him; and I know, my lord,
    If law, authority, and power deny not,
    It will go hard with poor Antonio.
Portia: Is it your dear friend that is thus in trouble?

291   *best-condition'd:* most able, most ready

292   *courtesies:* acts of kindness

293   *ancient Roman honour:* loyalty to friends and country

297   *deface:* cancel

308   *maids:* unmarried women

309   *shall hence:* shall go from here

311   *dear:* expensive; *Since you are . . . dear:* (What is Portia's pun?)

315   *forfeit:* overdue, past due

317-318 *use your pleasure:* do as you wish

320   *dispatch:* hurry to complete

323-324 *No bed . . . twain:* I shall not sleep, or even rest, until we are together again.

Bassanio: The dearest friend to me, the kindest man,   290
   The best-condition'd and unwearied spirit
   In doing courtesies, and one in whom
   The ancient Roman honour more appears
   Than any that draws breath in Italy.
Portia: What sum owes he the Jew?   295
Bassanio: For me, three thousand ducats.
Portia: What, no more?
   Pay him six thousand, and deface the bond;
   Double six thousand, and then treble that,
   Before a friend of this description
   Shall lose a hair through Bassanio's fault.   300
   First go with me to church and call me wife,
   And then away to Venice to your friend;
   For never shall you lie by Portia's side
   With an unquiet soul. You shall have gold
   To pay the petty debt twenty times over: 305
   When it is paid, bring your true friend along.
   My maid Nerissa and myself meantime
   Will live as maids and widows. Come, away!
   For you shall hence upon your wedding-day.
   Bid your friends welcome, show a merry cheer;   310
   Since you are dear bought, I will love you dear.
   But let me hear the letter of your friend.
Bassanio: Sweet Bassanio, my ships have all miscarried, my
   creditors grow cruel, my estate is very low, my bond to the
   Jew is forfeit; and since, in paying it, it is impossible I   315
   should live, all debts are cleared between you and I, if I
   might but see you at my death. Notwithstanding, use your
   pleasure; if your love do not persuade you to come, let not
   my letter.
Portia: O love, dispatch all business, and be gone!   320
Bassanio: Since I have your good leave to go away,
   I will make haste; but, till I come again,
   No bed shall e'er be guilty of my stay,
   Nor rest be interposer 'twixt us twain.   [*Exeunt*]

Act 3, Scene 2: Activities

1. The audience already knows before the scene begins that Portia's picture is in the leaden casket. As a director, you would have to decide whether this fact decreases the suspense in the first half of the scene. In your director's log, record the instructions you would give to the actors playing Portia and Bassanio to heighten the level of suspense for your audience. Consider positioning and movement of the actors on stage, variations in vocal rhythm and inflection, pauses in the action, and the use of facial expression and gesture. Record your decisions in your director's log.

2. How does Portia's first speech in the scene (lines 1–24) show us a side of her character we have not seen before? Is the Portia we see here consistent with the Portia we have seen in earlier scenes? How do you react to her at this point? Share your observations with a partner or in a small group.

3. Carefully reread the song in lines 63–72. Do you think it contains direct clues to the correct casket? Do you think that Portia has betrayed her promise to her father by calling for this song? Complete one of the following activities:

   a) In pairs, improvise or script a scene in which Portia justifies breaking the rules of the casket lottery to Nerissa. Be sure to include Nerissa's responses, realizing that she, too, has an interest in Bassanio's success.

   OR

   b) As Shakespeare, write a letter directed against critics who have charged that the inclusion of the song makes your romantic hero and heroine less than admirable people.

   OR

   c) As a director, decide whether you would include or cut the song in a full-scale production of the play. Outline the reasons for your decision in a director's log.

4. Do you consider the long speech in which Bassanio justifies his choice of the leaden casket (lines 73–107) to reflect a character consistent with the Bassanio we know? Consult the list of Bassanio's characteristics that you have been compiling. If Bassanio missed the clues in the song, how might you account for his newfound wisdom? If you believe he has understood the clues, why do you think he takes so long to make his choice?

   In a small group, discuss your responses to these three questions. Work toward a consensus on Bassanio's worthiness as Portia's victorious suitor.

   Record your own thoughts in a personal journal entry.

5. How does Portia's view of the perfect marriage (lines 149–174) compare with depictions of "happy couples" in contemporary media? Write a response either in prose or in verse that compares or contrasts Portia's views with your own.

6. In this scene, Shakespeare interweaves three main storylines or plots of his play: the casket plot, the bond plot, and the elopement plot. With a partner, devise a diagram or chart in which you show how these three plots connect with one another in this scene.

7. Imagine that you are the Duke of Venice. Shylock has been "plying you at morning and at night" to uphold his case against Antonio. You have called a meeting of your top advisers to discuss how to resolve the situation with the least possible damage to your own reputation and that of the city. With a group, improvise the meeting. Report your conclusions to the class.

For the next scene . . .

Have you ever tried to reason with someone who was overcome with emotion? Why is this such a difficult task? What are the chances of success? What advice would you give a friend if he or she were trying to reason with you when you were very upset?

Act 3, Scene 3

In this scene . . .

In accordance with Shylock's arrangements, Antonio
has been arrested and taken to debtor's prison. His
jailer will have to produce the prisoner when the court
calls for him. In the meantime, he has gone out walking
with Antonio. They meet Shylock who is angry that
Antonio has any freedom whatsoever, and Shylock
berates the jailer for allowing Antonio in the street.
Antonio attempts to reason with Shylock, but he cannot
moderate Shylock's vindictive hatred. Solanio cannot
believe that the Duke will uphold Shylock's claim to a
pound of Antonio's flesh. However, Antonio knows that
the Duke cannot cancel the bond without damaging
Venice's reputation as a just state in which the rights of
all traders are protected.

1   *look to him:* guard him carefully

9   *naughty:* worthless, wicked; *fond:* foolish
10   *abroad:* outside, in the streets (that is, away from the prison)

14   *dull-eyed:* stupid, easily misled

16   *intercessors:* go-betweens, pleaders

18   *impenetrable cur:* insensitive and unfeeling dog
19   *kept with:* lived among

20   *bootless:* useless

22   *deliver'd:* rescued; *forfeitures:* legal suits against debtors
23   *made moan:* cried for help

25   *grant this forfeiture to hold:* allow this suit to be upheld in court

Scene 3

Venice. A street.

Enter Shylock, Solanio, Antonio,
and Gaoler.

Shylock: Gaoler, look to him: tell not me of mercy;
   This is the fool that lent out money gratis:
   Gaoler, look to him.
Antonio: Hear me yet, good Shylock.
Shylock: I'll have my bond; speak not against my bond:
   I have sworn an oath that I will have my bond.   5
   Thou call'dst me dog before thou hadst a cause,
   But, since I am a dog, beware my fangs:
   The duke shall grant me justice. I do wonder,
   Thou naughty gaoler, that thou art so fond
   To come abroad with him at his request.   10
Antonio: I pray thee, hear me speak.
Shylock: I'll have my bond; I will not hear thee speak:
   I'll have my bond, and therefore speak no more.
   I'll not be made a soft and dull-eyed fool,
   To shake the head, relent, and sigh, and yield   15
   To Christian intercessors. Follow not;
   I'll have no speaking; I will have my bond.   *[Exit]*
Solanio: It is the most impenetrable cur
   That ever kept with men.
Antonio: Let him alone:
   I'll follow him no more with bootless prayers.   20
   He seeks my life; his reason well I know.
   I oft deliver'd from his forfeitures
   Many that have at times made moan to me;
   Therefore he hates me.
Solanio: I am sure the duke
   Will never grant this forfeiture to hold.   25

27 *commodity:* rights, privileges; *strangers:* foreigners, non-Venetians (including Jews). Even if Shylock had been born in Venice, he would not have been given the privilege of citizenship. Nonetheless, Venice was known for the personal freedom allowed to non-citizens within its borders.

29 *impeach:* discredit, cast doubt upon

31 *Consisteth of all nations:* Venice depended upon international trade for its wealth and power.

32 *bated:* reduced (in weight)

34 *bloody:* bloodthirsty

Antonio: The duke cannot deny the course of law:
    For the commodity that strangers have
    With us in Venice, if it be denied,
    Will much impeach the justice of the state,
    Since that the trade and profit of the city   30
    Consisteth of all nations. Therefore, go:
    These griefs and losses have so bated me,
    That I shall hardly spare a pound of flesh
    Tomorrow to my bloody creditor.
    Well, gaoler, on. Pray God, Bassanio come   35
    To see me pay his debt, and then I care not!   [*Exeunt*]

Act 3, Scene 3: Activities

1. Antonio thinks he knows why Shylock wants to destroy him (lines 21–24). Do you think the reason Antonio gives is enough to account for Shylock's malice? As the audience, what do you know about Shylock's motives that Antonio does not take into account?

   a) Make notes on your own conclusions to these questions. Be sure to review Shylock's earlier scenes to find the evidence that supports your conclusions.

   b) In a small group, use your notes to draw up a list of Shylock's principal motives for pursuing revenge on Antonio. Rank these motives in order of importance to Shylock. All members of your group must agree on the order of importance. This will require careful consideration and assessment of everyone's point of view. As a whole class, share and compare your lists.

2. Experiment with various ways of delivering Antonio's last sentence in this scene. How can you use pauses, stresses, inflections, and volume to convey different emotions behind Antonio's words? How do you think Antonio is really feeling about his friend Bassanio at this point? Write a short soliloquy to add to the end of the scene in which Antonio explores these emotions.

3. In a small group, rewrite this short scene in modern English and present it to the class live or on video. Retain the original setting and situation, but feel free to experiment with details, images, and language.

4. If you were directing a production of the play, would you keep this short scene or leave it out? Explain the reasons for your decision in a director's log.

For the next scenes . . .

"Any friend of yours is a friend of mine." What is the meaning of this traditional saying? What obligations does it place on friendship?

Act 3, Scenes 4 and 5

In these scenes . . .

Portia asks Lorenzo to look after her estate, telling him that she and Nerissa are retreating to a nunnery to pray for their husbands' safe return. In reality, they plan to follow Bassanio and Gratiano to Venice, disguised as men.

When Portia and Nerissa have gone, Launcelot, who has travelled to Belmont with his new master, teases Jessica about her unavoidable damnation to hell. Lorenzo joins in the fun, claiming that he will be as good a husband as Portia is a wife to Bassanio.

2   *conceit:* understanding

3   *amity:* friendship

7   *lover:* close friend

8-9   *you would be . . . enforce you:* you would be more proud of this special act of kindness than of your usual acts of common courtesy and charity

12   *waste:* pass, spend

13   *Whose souls . . . love:* who share a friendship to which each is equally committed. Pairs of working oxen are linked together by a wooden collar called a *yoke.*

14   *needs:* of necessity

15   *lineaments:* physical features or characteristics

17   *bosom lover:* best friend

19   *bestow'd:* spent

20   *the semblance of my soul:* Antonio (her soul itself would be Bassanio)

25   *husbandry and manage:* careful management

Scene 4

Belmont. A room in Portia's house.
Enter Portia, Nerissa, Lorenzo,
Jessica, and Balthazar.

Lorenzo: Madam, although I speak it in your presence,
   You have a noble and a true conceit
   Of god-like amity; which appears most strongly
   In bearing thus the absence of your lord.
   But if you knew to whom you show this honour,   5
   How true a gentleman you send relief,
   How dear a lover of my lord your husband,
   I know you would be prouder of the work
   Than customary bounty can enforce you.
Portia: I never did repent for doing good,   10
   Nor shall not now: for in companions
   That do converse and waste the time together,
   Whose souls do bear an equal yoke of love,
   There must be needs a like proportion
   Of lineaments, of manners, and of spirit;   15
   Which makes me think that this Antonio,
   Being the bosom lover of my lord,
   Must needs be like my lord, If it be so,
   How little is the cost I have bestow'd
   In purchasing the semblance of my soul   20
   From out the state of hellish cruelty!
   This comes too near the praising of myself;
   Therefore, no more of it: hear other things.
   Lorenzo, I commit into your hands
   The husbandry and manage of my house   25
   Until my lord's return: for mine own part,
   I have toward heaven breath'd a secret vow
   To live in prayer and contemplation,
   Only attended by Nerissa here,
   Until her husband and my lord's return.   30

33   *imposition:* request, duty

37   *My people:* my household servants

46   *ever:* always

49   *render:* give

50   *Doctor:* In Shakespeare's time, this title was applied to all of the professions. Doctor Bellario is, in fact, a lawyer, not a physician. At this time, the University of Padua enjoyed international fame as a centre of learning.

52   *with imagin'd speed:* as quickly as may be imagined

53   *traject:* wharf, dock. The medieval Italian word for a ferry is *traghetto.*

54   *trades:* travels back and forth

56   *all convenient speed:* as fast as I can

57   *in hand:* to be done

60   *habit:* costume

61   *accomplished:* equipped

62   *With that we lack:* with what we do not have

63   *accoutered:* dressed

66   *between the change . . . boy:* as if my voice were breaking

67   *reed:* squeaky; *mincing:* dainty

There is a monastery two miles off,
And there we will abide. I do desire you
Not to deny this imposition,
The which my love and some necessity
Now lays upon you.   35
Lorenzo: Madam, with all my heart:
   I shall obey you in all fair commands.
Portia: My people do already know my mind,
   And will acknowledge you and Jessica
   In place of Lord Bassanio and myself.
   So fare you well till we shall meet again.   40
Lorenzo: Fair thoughts and happy hours attend on you!
Jessica: I wish your ladyship all heart's content.
Portia: I thank you for your wish, and am well pleas'd
   To wish it back on you: fare you well, Jessica.
                               [*Exeunt Jessica and Lorenzo*]
   Now, Balthazar,   45
   As I have ever found thee honest-true,
   So let me find thee still. Take this same letter,
   And use thou all th' endeavour of a man
   In speed to Padua: see thou render this
   Into my cousin's hand, Doctor Bellario;   50
   And look what notes and garments he doth give thee,
   Bring them, I pray thee, with imagin'd speed
   Unto the traject, to the common ferry
   Which trades to Venice. Waste no time in words,
   But get thee gone: I shall be there before thee.   55
Balthazar: Madam, I go with all convenient speed.   [*Exit*]
Portia: Come on, Nerissa: I have work in hand
   That you yet know not of: we'll see our husbands
   Before they think of us.
Nerissa: Shall they see us?
Portia: They shall, Nerissa; but in such a habit   60
   That they shall think we are accomplished
   With that we lack. I'll hold thee any wager,
   When we are both accoutered like young men,
   I'll prove the prettier fellow of the two,
   And wear my dagger with the braver grace,   65
   And speak between the change of man and boy
   With a reed voice, and turn two mincing steps

68   *frays:* fights, quarrels

69   *quaint:* ingenious, elaborate

72   *I could not do withal:* I could do nothing to help it.

74   *puny:* feeble

77   *raw:* youthful, crude; *bragging Jacks:* boastful men

78   *turn to men:* turn ourselves into men. Portia pretends to take
      the meaning differently.

80   *lewd:* dirty-minded

81   *device:* plan

Into a manly stride, and speak of frays
Like a fine bragging youth, and tell quaint lies,
How honourable ladies sought my love,   70
Which I denying, they fell sick and died—
I could not do withal; then I'll repent,
And wish, for all that, that I had not kill'd them.
And twenty of these puny lies I'll tell,
That men shall swear I have discontinu'd school   75
Above a twelvemonth. I have within my mind
A thousand raw tricks of these bragging Jacks,
Which I will practise.
Nerissa: Why, shall we turn to men?
Portia: Fie, what a question's that,
If thou wert near a lewd interpreter!   80
But come: I'll tell thee all my whole device
When I am in my coach, which stays for us
At the park gate; and therefore haste away,
For we must measure twenty miles today.   [*Exeunt*]

1   *look you:* you see

1-2   *the sins . . . children:* Children pay the penalties for their fathers' sins according to the Ten Commandments (*Exodus* 20:5).

3   *I fear you:* I fear for you, I am concerned about your welfare; *plain:* honest

4   *agitation:* Launcelot means *cogitation* (thought, opinion).

7   *bastard hope:* false hope. Launcelot's pun expresses his true hope that Jessica may not be Shylock's legitimate daughter.

9-10   *got you not:* did not beget (father) you

11-12   *so the sins . . . upon me:* Therefore, I would be punished for the sins of my mother (that is, adultery).

14-15   *Scylla . . . Charybdis:* In Greek mythology, these are witches of the shoals. To go near Scylla (reefs) is as dangerous as approaching Charybdis (whirlpool)—our "between a rock and a hard place." Therefore, there are two dangers, in that to avoid one increases the risk of confronting the other.

15   *gone:* doomed, lost

17   *I shall be . . . husband:* For the Biblical allusion, see *I Corinthians* 7:12–14. According to St. Paul, an unbelieving wife is "saved" by a believing husband, and an unbelieving husband can be "saved" by a believing wife.

19-21   *we were Christians . . . one by another:* There were enough Christians before he converted you, just enough of us to live comfortably together.

21-22   *This making of Christians . . . hogs:* Launcelot is wise enough to understand the economic laws of supply and demand. He is also aware that the dietary laws of the Old Testament forbid the eating of pork. See Shylock's vow in Act 1, Scene 3, lines 30–31.

22-23   *we shall not . . . money:* soon we will not be able to buy bacon at any price

27   *corners:* secret or private places

28-29   *Launcelot and I are out:* We have had a quarrel.

Scene 5

Belmont. Portia's garden.
Enter Launcelot and Jessica.

Launcelot: Yes, truly; for, look you, the sins of the father
are to be laid upon the children; therefore, I promise
you, I fear you. I was always plain with you, and so
now I speak my agitation of the matter: therefore be
o' good cheer; for, truly, I think you are damned.   5
There is but one hope in it that can do you any good,
and that is but a kind of bastard hope neither.
Jessica: And what hope is that, I pray thee?
Launcelot: Marry, you may partly hope that your father got
you not, that you are not the Jew's daughter.   10
Jessica: That were a kind of bastard hope, indeed: so the
sins of my mother should be visited upon me.
Launcelot: Truly then I fear you are damned both by father
and mother: thus when I shun Scylla (your father) I
fall into Charybdis (your mother): well, you are gone   15
both ways.
Jessica: I shall be saved by my husband; he hath made me
a Christian.
Launcelot: Truly the more to blame he: we were Christians
enow before; e'en as many as could well live one by   20
another. This making of Christians will raise the price
of hogs: if we grow all to be pork-eaters, we shall not
shortly have a rasher on the coals for money.
    [*Enter Lorenzo*]
Jessica: I'll tell my husband, Launcelot, what you say: here
he comes.   25
Lorenzo: I shall grow jealous of you shortly, Launcelot, if
you thus get my wife into corners.
Jessica: Nay, you need not fear us, Lorenzo: Launcelot and
I are out. He tells me flatly there's no mercy for me in
heaven, because I am a Jew's daughter: and he says   30

31   *commonwealth:* state

34   *answer:* explain, justify

35   *getting up:* swelling

37   *Moor:* Moroccan woman (perhaps a servant in Portia's household)

37-38   *more than reason:* bigger than reasonable, bigger than she should be. Launcelot's pun depends upon the Elizabethan pronunciation of *Moor* as *more.*

38   *honest:* virtuous

41-42   *the best grace . . . parrots:* the best way to display one's intelligence will be to remain silent, and only parrots will be admired for their speaking

44   *they all have stomachs:* they are all hungry

45   *wit-snapper:* wisecracker

48   *cover:* set the table. The dinner has been prepared for some time already. In line 56, Launcelot jokingly misinterprets Lorenzo's repetition of the word *cover* as *put on your hat.* Launcelot would take his hat off as a sign of respect.

50   *quarrelling with occasion:* playing with words or quibbling at every opportunity

57   *humours and conceits:* whims and fancies

59   *discretion:* careful selection (of words)

62   *A many:* many; *stand in better place:* have better positions

63   *Garnish'd:* both "supplied" (with words) and "dressed" (in his serving liveries); *for:* for the sake of

64   *Defy the matter:* confuse the issue; *How cheer'st thou:* Are you happy?

67   *Past all expressing:* More than I could say. *meet:* appropriate

68   *upright:* honourable

you are no good member of the commonwealth, for, in
converting Jews to Christians, you raise the price of
pork.

Lorenzo: I shall answer that better to the commonwealth
than you can the getting up of the negro's belly: the   35
Moor is with child by you, Launcelot.

Launcelot: It is much that the Moor should be more than
reason; but if she be less than an honest woman, she
is indeed more than I took her for.

Lorenzo: How every fool can play upon the word! I think   40
the best grace of wit will shortly turn into silence, and
discourse grow commendable in none only but parrots.
Go in, sirrah: bid them prepare for dinner.

Launcelot: That is done, sir; they have all stomachs.

Lorenzo: Goodly Lord, what a wit-snapper are you! then   45
bid them prepare dinner.

Launcelot: That is done too, sir; only 'cover' is the word.

Lorenzo: Will you cover, then, sir?

Launcelot: Not so, sir, neither; I know my duty.

Lorenzo: Yet more quarrelling with occasion! Wilt thou show 50
the whole wealth of thy wit in an instant? I pray thee,
understand a plain man in his plain meaning: go to
thy fellows; bid them cover the table, serve in the
meat, and we will come in to dinner.

Launcelot: For the table, sir, it shall be served in; for the 55
meat, sir, it shall be covered; for your coming in to
dinner, sir, why, let it be as humours and conceits
shall govern.   [*Exit*]

Lorenzo: O dear discretion, how his words are suited!
The fool hath planted in his memory   60
An army of good words, and I do know
A many fools, that stand in better place,
Garnish'd like him, that for a tricksy word
Defy the matter. How cheer'st thou, Jessica?
And now, good sweet, say thy opinion;   65
How dost thou like the Lord Bassanio's wife?

Jessica: Past all expressing. It is very meet
The Lord Bassanio live an upright life,
For, having such a blessing in his lady,
He finds the joys of heaven here on earth;   70

72   *In reason:* it makes sense that

74   *on the wager lay:* place as their bet

76   *Pawn'd:* bet
77   *fellow:* equal

80   *anon:* soon
81   *stomach:* desire (both to eat and to praise you)

83   *howsome'er:* in whatever manner

84   *I'll set you forth:* I'll serve it to you. Jessica continues the metaphor of praise as food.

And if on earth he do not merit it,
In reason he should never come to heaven.
Why, if two gods should play some heavenly match,
And on the wager lay two earthly women,
And Portia one, there must be something else   75
Pawn'd with the other, for the poor rude world
Hath not her fellow.
Lorenzo: Even such a husband
Hast thou of me, as she is for a wife.
Jessica: Nay, but ask my opinion too of that.
Lorenzo: I will anon; first, let us go to dinner.   80
Jessica: Nay, let me praise you while I have a stomach.
Lorenzo: No, pray thee, let it serve for table-talk;
Then howsome'er thou speak'st, 'mong other things
I shall digest it.
Jessica: Well, I'll set you forth.

                                 [*Exeunt*]

Act 3, Scenes 4 and 5: Activities

1. There are many possible variations in acting the role of Portia. In pairs, prepare two readings (one by each of you) of her speech on friendship (Scene 4, lines 10–23).

   Your two readings should present two different interpretations of Portia's character. She might sound sincere and generous, hypocritical and selfish, or even sarcastic.

   Whatever characteristics you choose to develop, your main tool should be your voice. Experiment with variations in pace, pitch, volume, and tone, as well as the use of pauses.

   Tape your readings or present them live to your class. Allow time for your classmates to compare their responses to your different versions of Portia. Discuss which versions are most convincing in light of the play's action so far.

2. Portia prepares us for an unexpected turn of events in her speeches to Balthazar and Nerissa in Scene 4. Put the clues together and predict the circumstances under which we will meet Portia and Nerissa again. Record your predictions in your journal, and check them for accuracy when you have completed your reading of the play.

3. Scene 5 provides a second view of Launcelot and Jessica in a "domestic" setting. In a group of three, list the important differences between this scene in Portia's house and the earlier scene outside Shylock's house (Act 2, Scene 5). Consider such features as the following:

   • humour

   • dramatic tone (mood of the scene)

   • characters' relationships

   • action

   • language use and word play

   Use this list to clarify how this scene supports Jessica's decision to leave her father's house and Launcelot's decision to leave Shylock's service.

4. If you were designing costumes for Lorenzo and Jessica in these two scenes, how would they differ and why? Prepare sketches for the two scenes, providing a short explanation of your choices. These notes may be written in the margin next to your drawings.

For the next scenes . . .

How do judges maintain order in court? Why do they sometimes have difficulty with courtroom order? Why do lawyers raise objections to proceedings on behalf of their clients? How do lawyers sometimes go beyond the boundaries of proper courtroom behaviour?

Act 4, Scenes 1 and 2

In these scenes . . .

In the courtroom, Shylock demands that Antonio pay the penalty for failing to return the borrowed money on time. The Duke of Venice, who is acting as the judge in the case, encourages Shylock to show mercy to Antonio, but Shylock refuses. Bassanio offers to repay Shylock more than the sum Antonio borrowed, but Antonio has prepared himself to accept defeat—and death.

As Shylock is sharpening his knife to cut the pound of flesh from Antonio's breast, Portia arrives in court, disguised as Balthazar, a young but learned Doctor of Law. Portia renews the Duke's plea for mercy, but Shylock remains adamant. Without further delay, Portia decrees that Shylock is legally entitled to the pound of flesh. However, just as Shylock is about to take his revenge, Portia clarifies the exact wording of the bond, and Shylock's plan is defeated. Portia then points out that, under the law, Shylock should be punished for his attempt to injure Antonio. She insists that the court follow *the letter of the law* and show no mercy to Shylock, since he has been so insistent himself in carrying out the penalty agreed upon with Antonio. However, both the Duke and Antonio show mercy to Shylock as the trial comes to an end.

In gratitude for saving Antonio, Bassanio offers to give the young lawyer a gift. Portia demands his wedding ring. At first Bassanio refuses, with much embarrassment, but Antonio encourages him to give the ring up. Nerissa, disguised as Balthazar's clerk, also plans a way to trick Gratiano into giving his wedding ring to her.

5   *void:* empty. Note the repetition for emphasis.

6   *dram:* small drop

7   *qualify:* modify, moderate

8   *obdurate:* stubborn, relentless

9-10   *And that no . . . envy's reach:* and I cannot be protected
        from his malice (*envy*) by the law

11   *arm'd:* prepared

13   *tyranny:* violence

16   *before our face:* in front of me. The plural pronoun was com-
        monly used by royalty in Shakespeare's time.

18-19   *That thou . . . hour of act:* that you intend to make a show of
        relentless cruelty until the last possible moment

20   *remorse:* compassion, pity

21   *apparent:* seeming

22   *exact'st:* demand

24   *loose:* release, forget; *forfeiture:* penalty

26   *Forgive:* allow (Antonio) to keep; *moiety:* portion

Act 4, Scene 1

Venice. A court of justice.

Enter the Duke, the Merchants,
Antonio, Bassanio, Gratiano,
Salerio, and Officers of the Court.

Duke: What, is Antonio here?
Antonio: Ready, so please your Grace.
Duke: I am sorry for thee: thou art come to answer
    A stony adversary, an inhuman wretch
    Uncapable of pity, void and empty   5
    From any dram of mercy.
Antonio: I have heard
    Your Grace hath ta'en great pains to qualify
    His rigorous course; but since he stands obdurate,
    And that no lawful means can carry me
    Out of his envy's reach, I do oppose   10
    My patience to his fury, and am arm'd
    To suffer with a quietness of spirit
    The very tyranny and rage of his.
Duke: Go one, and call the Jew into the court.
Salerio: He is ready at the door: he comes, my lord.   15
    [*Enter Shylock*]
Duke: Make room, and let him stand before our face.
    Shylock, the world thinks, and I think so too,
    That thou but lead'st this fashion of thy malice
    To the last hour of act; and then 'tis thought
    Thou'lt show thy mercy and remorse more strange   20
    Than is thy strange apparent cruelty;
    And where thou now exact'st the penalty—
    Which is a pound of this poor merchant's flesh—
    Thou wilt not only loose the forfeiture,
    But, touch'd with human gentleness and love,   25
    Forgive a moiety of the principal,

29   *Enow:* enough

30   *commiseration of:* sympathy for

31   *brassy bosoms:* hearts as hard and as cold as brass

32   *Turks:* From medieval times until the early twentieth century, Turks were considered by Europeans to be savage and cruel. This stereotype may have been based on widespread reports of the cruel practices of the Ottoman Empire.

      Tartars: The Asiatic tribes of this name are correctly called *Tatars*. Shakespeare's change probably reflects an association with Tartarus (Hades or Hell) in classical mythology. The Tatars, who travelled with Genghis Khan, were reputed to be among the most savage of men.

32-33 *train'd To offices of:* taught to practise

35   *possess'd:* informed

36   *Sabbath:* the holiest day of the week, reserved for rest and prayer, as commanded by God in the Ten Commandments (*Exodus* 20:8–11). For Shylock, the Sabbath would be Saturday rather than Sunday, which is the Christian Sabbath.

37   *due and forfeit:* proper penalty

38   *light:* descend, fall

39   *charter:* authority

41   *carrion:* rotten

43   *humour:* whim, fancy

46   *ban'd: baned* (poisoned), not *banned*

47   *gaping pig:* a roasted pig with an open mouth (often stuffed with an apple)

49   *sings i' the nose:* drones (with a nasal tone)

50   *affection:* inclination, impulse

54-56 *he . . . he . . . he:* one man . . . another man . . . a third man

56   *woollen:* the leather bag of the Highland bagpipe is commonly wrapped in cotton or flannel

56-58 *but of force . . . being offended:* but he cannot prevent giving offence (that is, urinating in public) when he himself has been offended (by the bagpipe)

62   *A losing suit:* By pursuing the pound of flesh, Shylock will lose the money he lent to Antonio.

64   *current of thy cruelty:* the course that your cruelty is taking

Glancing an eye of pity on his losses,
That have of late so huddled on his back,
Enow to press a royal merchant down,
And pluck commiseration of his state   30
From brassy bosoms and rough hearts of flint,
From stubborn Turks and Tartars, never train'd
To offices of tender courtesy.
We all expect a gentle answer, Jew.
Shylock: I have possess'd your Grace of what I purpose;   35
And by our holy Sabbath have I sworn
To have the due and forfeit of my bond:
If you deny it, let the danger light
Upon your charter and your city's freedom.
You'll ask me, why I rather choose to have   40
A weight of carrion flesh than to receive
Three thousand ducats. I'll not answer that,
But say it is my humour. Is it answer'd?
What if my house be troubled with a rat,
And I be pleas'd to give ten thousand ducats   45
To have it ban'd? What, are you answer'd yet?
Some men there are love not a gaping pig;
Some, that are mad if they behold a cat;
And others, when the bagpipe sings i' the nose,
Cannot contain their urine: for affection,   50
Master of passion, sways it to the mood
Of what it likes, or loathes. Now, for your answer:
As there is no firm reason to be render'd,
Why he cannot abide a gaping pig;
Why he, a harmless necessary cat;   55
Why he, a woollen bagpipe, but of force
Must yield to such inevitable shame
As to offend, himself being offended;
So can I give no reason, nor I will not,
More than a lodg'd hate and a certain loathing   60
I bear Antonio, that I follow thus
A losing suit against him. Are you answer'd?
Bassanio: This is no answer, thou unfeeling man,
To excuse the current of thy cruelty.
Shylock: I am not bound to please thee with my answers. 65
Bassanio: Do all men kill the things they do not love?

68   *Every . . . first:* A single annoyance is not justifiable cause for hatred.

70   *think you question with:* remember that you are arguing with

72   *main flood:* high tide; *bate:* abate, reduce

73   *use question with:* ask

74   *ewe:* mother sheep; *bleat:* cry

76   *wag:* wave

77   *fretten:* fretted, blown

82   *conveniency:* efficiency

87   *draw:* accept

90   *You have . . . purchas'd slave:* Shylock's reference to slavery in Europe is intended to draw a comparison, not to question the practice of slavery itself. His point merely emphasizes the right of a property owner to use his property as he wishes.

92   *in abject . . . parts:* for base and servile jobs

97   *viands:* delicacies

100   *dearly:* at great expense

102   *force:* power, enforcement; *decrees:* laws, decisions

104   *Upon:* in accordance with

105   *doctor:* lawyer (See the note for Act 3, Scene 4, line 50.)

106   *determine:* decide, settle

Shylock: Hates any man the thing he would not kill?
Bassanio: Every offence is not a hate at first.
Shylock: What! wouldst thou have a serpent sting thee twice?
Antonio: I pray you, think you question with the Jew: 70
    You may as well go stand upon the beach,
    And bid the main flood bate his usual height;
    You may as well use question with the wolf,
    Why he hath made the ewe bleat for the lamb;
    You may as well forbid the mountain pines   75
    To wag their high tops, and to make no noise
    When they are fretten with the gusts of heaven;
    You may as well do anything most hard,
    As seek to soften that—than which what's harder?—
    His Jewish heart: therefore, I do beseech you,   80
    Make no more offers, use no farther means;
    But with all brief and plain conveniency,
    Let me have judgment, and the Jew his will.
Bassanio: For thy three thousand ducats here is six.
Shylock: If every ducat in six thousand ducats   85
    Were in six parts, and every part a ducat,
    I would not draw them. I would have my bond.
Duke: How shalt thou hope for mercy, rendering none?
Shylock: What judgment shall I dread, doing no wrong?
    You have among you many a purchas'd slave,   90
    Which, like your asses and your dogs and mules,
    You use in abject and in slavish parts,
    Because you bought them: shall I say to you,
    'Let them be free, marry them to your heirs?
    Why sweat they under burdens? let their beds   95
    Be made as soft as yours, and let their palates
    Be season'd with such viands?' You will answer,
    'The slaves are ours'. So do I answer you:
    The pound of flesh which I demand of him,
    Is dearly bought; 'tis mine and I will have it.   100
    If you deny me, fie upon your law!
    There is no force in the decrees of Venice.
    I stand for judgment. Answer—shall I have it?
Duke: Upon my power I may dismiss this court,
    Unless Bellario, a learned doctor,   105
    Whom I have sent for to determine this,

109   *New:* recently, just this minute

114   *tainted:* diseased; *wether:* castrated ram

115   *Meetest:* most suitable

118   *live still:* continue living; *epitaph:* inscription on a tombstone, often in praise of the deceased person

121   *whet:* sharpen. The lines that follow indicate that Shylock is using the leather sole of his shoe to sharpen his knife.

124   *keen:* sharp

125   *hangman:* executioner. Beheading, rather than hanging, was the most common form of capital punishment in Shakespeare's day. *Hangman* was a term used for an executioner of any type.

126   *envy:* malice, hatred

128   *inexecrable:* unable to be cursed. Gratiano suggests that Shylock is so evil that no curse adequately condemns him.

129   *for thy life . . . accus'd:* It is unjust that you are allowed to live. (Justice deserves to be found guilty for allowing you to live.)

130   *my faith:* Gratiano's faith is Christianity, which does not allow a belief in reincarnation.

131   *hold opinion:* agree; *Pythagoras:* Pythagoras was a Greek philosopher and mathematician of the sixth century B.C. who believed that the souls of the dead were reborn in the bodies of other humans or animals. This belief directly opposes both the Christian and Jewish faiths. His skills as a mathematician led to the discovery of the geometric law known today as the Pythagorean theorem.

132   *infuse:* pour

133   *trunks:* bodies; *currish:* like a cur (mongrel dog)

134   *hang'd for human slaughter:* In Shakespeare's time, animals suspected of killing or attacking humans were actually hanged.

135   *Even:* directly; *fell:* cruel; *fleet:* fly away

136   *unhallow'd:* unholy (un-Christian); *dam:* mother

139   *rail:* shout, rant

140   *offend'st:* injure

143   *commend:* recommend

Come here today.
Salerio:　　　　　　My lord, here stays without
　A messenger with letters from the doctor,
　New come from Padua.
Duke: Bring us the letters: call the messenger.　　　　　110
Bassanio: Good cheer, Antonio! What, man, courage yet!
　The Jew shall have my flesh, blood, bones, and all,
　Ere thou shalt lose for me one drop of blood.
Antonio: I am a tainted wether of the flock,
　Meetest for death: the weakest kind of fruit　　　　　115
　Drops earliest to the ground; and so let me.
　You cannot better be employ'd, Bassanio,
　Than to live still, and write mine epitaph.
　[*Enter Nerissa, dressed like a lawyer's clerk*]
Duke: Came you from Padua, from Bellario?
Nerissa: From both, my lord. Bellario greets your Grace.　　120
　　　　　　　　　　　　　[*Presents a letter*]
Bassanio: Why dost thou whet thy knife so earnestly?
Shylock: To cut the forfeiture from that bankrupt there.
Gratiano: Not on thy sole, but on thy soul, harsh Jew,
　Thou mak'st thy knife keen; but no metal can,
　No, not the hangman's axe, bear half the keenness　　125
　Of thy sharp envy. Can no prayers pierce thee?
Shylock: No, none that thou hast wit enough to make.
Gratiano: O, be thou damn'd, inexecrable dog!
　And for thy life let justice be accus'd.
　Thou almost mak'st me waver in my faith　　　　　130
　To hold opinion with Pythagoras,
　That souls of animals infuse themselves
　Into the trunks of men: thy currish spirit
　Govern'd a wolf, who, hang'd for human slaughter,
　Even from the gallows did his fell soul fleet,　　　　135
　And whilst thou lay'st in thy unhallow'd dam,
　Infus'd itself in thee; for thy desires
　Are wolvish, bloody, starv'd, and ravenous.
Shylock: Till thou canst rail the seal from off my bond.
　Thou but offend'st thy lungs to speak so loud:　　　140
　Repair thy wit, good youth, or it will fall
　To cureless ruin. I stand here for law.
Duke: This letter from Bellario doth commend

145   *hard by:* nearby

148   *conduct:* escort

153   *cause:* case, matter

155   *turned o'er:* looked through

155-156 *is furnish'd with:* has been given

156   *bettered:* improved

158   *importunity:* request

159   *in my stead:* in my place

159-161 *let his lack . . . reverend estimation:* do not let his youth be an obstacle to your high opinion of him

162-163 *trial . . . commendation:* When you use him, you will discover how much his worth exceeds my praise.

168   *difference:* dispute

170   *throughly:* thoroughly (Other than impartiality, why would she pretend? And we do not believe she does. The special "costume" for Shylock actually was not required in Venice.)

175   *in such rule:* so within the law

176   *impugn:* find fault with, oppose

A young and learned doctor to our court.
Where is he? 145
Nerissa: He attendeth here hard by,
   To know your answer, whether you'll admit him.
Duke: With all my heart: some three or four of you
   Go give him courteous conduct to this place.
                         [*Exeunt Officers*]
   Meantime, the court shall hear Bellario's letter.

Your Grace shall understand that at the receipt of your letter 150
I am very sick; but in the instant that your messenger came,
in loving visitation was with me a young doctor of Rome;
his name is Balthazar. I acquainted him with the cause
in controversy between the Jew and Antonio the
merchant. We turned o'er many books together. He is 155
furnished with my opinion; which, bettered with his own
learning—the greatness whereof I cannot enough
commend—comes with him, at my importunity, to fill up
your Grace's request in my stead. I beseech you, let his
lack of years be no impediment to let him lack a reverend 160
estimation, for I never knew so young a body with so old
a head. I leave him to your gracious acceptance, whose trial
shall better publish his commendation.

[*Enter Portia, dressed like a doctor of law*]
   You hear the learn'd Bellario, what he writes:
   And here, I take it, is the doctor come. 165
   Give me your hand. Come you from old Bellario?
Portia: I did, my lord.
Duke: You are welcome: take your place.
   Are you acquainted with the difference
   That holds this present question in the court?
Portia: I am informed throughly of the cause. 170
   Which is the merchant here, and which the Jew?
Duke: Antonio and old Shylock, both stand forth.
Portia: Is your name Shylock?
Shylock: Shylock is my name.
Portia: Of a strange nature is the suit you follow;
   Yet in such rule, that the Venetian law 175
   Cannot impugn you as you do proceed.

177   *within his danger:* in his power

179   *Then must . . . merciful:* Portia suggests to Antonio that
        Shylock's mercy is his only hope. Shylock's interruption indi-
        cates that he interprets her use of the word *must* as a com-
        mand.

180   *On what . . . that:* What will force me to be merciful?

181   *quality:* trait, virtue, human characteristic; *is not strain'd:* can-
        not be forced

183   *it is twice bless'd:* it blesses twice

185   *becomes:* suits

187   *shows:* represents, symbolizes; *temporal:* earthly, in time
        (that is, not eternal)

188   *attribute to:* symbol of

189   *Wherein . . . kings:* When we see the king's sceptre, we are
        reminded of his authority over us and, therefore, respect and
        fear his power.

190   *above this sceptred sway:* is greater than the temporal
        power represented by the sceptre

194   *seasons:* moderates

195   *Though . . . plea:* although you are asking for justice

196-197 *That in the course . . . mercy:* If God pursued justice without
        mercy (as you do), no man or woman would be saved (from
        eternal damnation).

200   *mitigate:* soften, moderate

203   *My deeds upon my head:* I take full responsibility for what I
        am doing; *crave:* demand

205   *discharge:* repay

206   *tender:* offer

208   *I will be bound:* I will sign a legal agreement

211   *bears down:* crushes, destroys

212   *Wrest:* twist, bend; *once:* on this one occasion; *to:* with

214   *curb:* restrain

[*To Antonio*] You stand within his danger, do you not?
Antonio: Ay, so he says.
Portia: Do you confess the bond?
Antonio: I do.
Portia: Then must the Jew be merciful.
Shylock: On what compulsion must I? tell me that.   180
Portia: The quality of mercy is not strain'd;
   It droppeth as the gentle rain from heaven
   Upon the place beneath: it is twice bless'd;
   It blesseth him that gives and him that takes.
   'Tis mightiest in the mightiest: it becomes   185
   The throned monarch better than his crown;
   His sceptre shows the force of temporal power,
   The attribute to awe and majesty,
   Wherein doth sit the dread and fear of kings:
   But mercy is above this sceptred sway,   190
   It is enthroned in the hearts of kings,
   It is an attribute to God himself,
   And earthly power doth then show likest God's
   When mercy seasons justice. Therefore, Jew,
   Though justice be thy plea, consider this,   195
   That in the course of justice none of us
   Should see salvation: we do pray for mercy,
   And that same prayer doth teach us all to render
   The deeds of mercy. I have spoke thus much
   To mitigate the justice of thy plea,   200
   Which if thou follow, this strict court of Venice
   Must needs give sentence 'gainst the merchant there.
Shylock: My deeds upon my head! I crave the law,
   The penalty and forfeit of my bond.
Portia: Is he not able to discharge the money?   205
Bassanio: Yes, here I tender it for him in the court;
   Yea, twice the sum: if that will not suffice,
   I will be bound to pay it ten times o'er,
   On forfeit of my hands, my head, my heart.
   If this will not suffice, it must appear   210
   That malice bears down truth. And, I beseech you,
   Wrest once the law to your authority:
   To do a great right, do a little wrong,
   And curb this cruel devil of his will.

220   *Daniel:* A Daniel is one who displays wisdom beyond his years. *The Story of Susannah* tells how Susannah rejected the advances of two elders, was falsely accused by them, and was condemned to death. They claimed to have seen her lying under a tree with a young man. Daniel established Susannah's innocence—and the hypocrisy of the elders—by asking each accuser separately under what kind of tree the adultery had taken place. Each named a different tree.

225   *An oath:* Shylock means the oath referred to in lines 36–39.

232   *tenour:* wording or details (of a legal document)

234   *exposition:* interpretation, explanation

245   *Hath full relation to:* supports fully

248   *elder:* more mature (hence, wiser)

Portia: It must not be. There is no power in Venice   215
    Can alter a decree established:
    'Twill be recorded for a precedent,
    And many an error by the same example
    Will rush into the state. It cannot be.
Shylock: A Daniel come to judgment! yea, a Daniel!   220
    O wise young judge, how I do honour thee!
Portia: I pray you, let me look upon the bond.
Shylock: Here 'tis, most reverend doctor, here it is.
Portia: Shylock, there's thrice thy money offer'd thee.
Shylock: An oath, an oath, I have an oath in heaven;   225
    Shall I lay perjury upon my soul?
    No, not for Venice.
Portia: Why, this bond is forfeit;
    And lawfully by this the Jew may claim
    A pound of flesh, to be by him cut off
    Nearest the merchant's heart. Be merciful: 230
    Take thrice thy money; bid me tear the bond.
Shylock: When it is paid according to the tenour.
    It doth appear you are a worthy judge;
    You know the law, your exposition
    Hath been most sound: I charge you by the law,   235
    Whereof you are a well-deserving pillar,
    Proceed to judgment: by my soul I swear
    There is no power in the tongue of man
    To alter me. I stay here on my bond.
    Most heartily I do beseech the court   240
    To give the judgment.
Portia: Why then, thus it is:
    You must prepare your bosom for his knife.
Shylock: O noble judge! O excellent young man!
Portia: For, the intent and purpose of the law
    Hath full relation to the penalty,   245
    Which here appeareth due upon the bond.
Shylock: 'Tis very true! O wise and upright judge!
    How much more elder art thou than thy looks!
Portia: Therefore lay bare your bosom.
Shylock: Ay, 'his breast':
    So says the bond:—doth it not, noble judge?—   250
    'Nearest his heart'—those are the very words.

252   *balance:* scales

254   *on your charge:* at your expense

256   *nominated:* specified

258   *for charity:* out of goodness

264   *Fortune:* Fors Fortuna was the classical goddess of chance
       or luck. In medieval times, she was usually pictured with her
       wheel of fortune.

265   *still her use:* her usual habit

268   *An age of poverty:* a poverty-stricken old age; *penance:*
       punishment

272   *speak me fair in death:* Speak kindly of me when I am dead.

275   *Repent:* regret

279-294 *Antonio . . . Christian!:* (What might be Shakespeare's
        purposes for this digression?)

280   *Which:* who

284   *deliver:* save

286   *by:* nearby

288   *I would she were in heaven:* To be in heaven, of course,
       Nerissa would have to be dead!

Portia: It is so. Are there balance here to weigh
   The flesh?
Shylock: I have them ready.
Portia: Have by some surgeon, Shylock, on your charge,
   To stop his wounds, lest he do bleed to death.   255
Shylock: Is it so nominated in the bond?
Portia: It is not so express'd; but what of that?
   'Twere good you do so much for charity.
Shylock: I cannot find it: 'tis not in the bond.
Portia: You, merchant, have you anything to say?   260
Antonio: But little: I am arm'd and well prepar'd.
   Give me your hand, Bassanio: fare you well!
   Grieve not that I am fall'n to this for you,
   For herein Fortune shows herself more kind
   Than is her custom: it is still her use   265
   To let the wretched man outlive his wealth,
   To view with hollow eye and wrinkled brow
   An age of poverty; from which lingering penance
   Of such misery doth she cut me off.
   Commend me to your honourable wife.   270
   Tell her the process of Antonio's end;
   Say how I lov'd you, speak me fair in death;
   And, when the tale is told, bid her be judge
   Whether Bassanio had not once a love.
   Repent but you that you shall lose your friend,   275
   And he repents not that he pays your debt;
   For if the Jew do cut but deep enough,
   I'll pay it instantly with all my heart.
Bassanio: Antonio, I am married to a wife
   Which is as dear to me as life itself;   280
   But life itself, my wife, and all the world,
   Are not with me esteem'd above thy life:
   I would lose all, ay, sacrifice them all,
   Here to this devil, to deliver you.
Portia: Your wife would give you little thanks for that,   285
   If she were by to hear you make the offer.
Gratiano: I have a wife, who, I protest, I love:
   I would she were in heaven, so she could
   Entreat some power to change this currish Jew.
Nerissa: 'Tis well you offer it behind her back;   290

293   *stock:* breed; *Barrabas:* Barrabas was the thief who was released instead of Jesus (*Matthew* 27:15–23) at Passover. Shakespeare's spelling points to the appropriate metrical pronunciation (with the accent on the first syllable).

295   *trifle:* waste; *pursue sentence:* proceed to a decision

302   *Tarry:* wait

303   *jot:* drop

308   *confiscate:* confiscated, taken as a legal penalty

311   *act:* written decree

312   *urgest:* demand

317   *Soft!:* roughly, "Slow down!" or "Keep quiet!"

318   *all:* nothing but

320   *upright:* honest

323   *just:* exactly

324   *just:* exact

325   *substance:* weight

327   *scruple:* a very small unit of weight, specifically 20 grains of an apothecary's (a pharmacist's or druggist's) measure.

328   *estimation:* amount (here, width)

The wish would make else an unquiet house.

Shylock: These be the Christian husbands! I have a daughter;
   Would any of the stock of Barrabas
   Had been her husband rather than a Christian!
   We trifle time; I pray thee, pursue sentence.   295

Portia: A pound of that same merchant's flesh is thine:
   The court awards it, and the law doth give it.

Shylock: Most rightful judge!

Portia: And you must cut this flesh from off his breast:
   The law allows it, and the court awards it.   300

Shylock: Most learned judge! A sentence! come, prepare!

Portia: Tarry a little: there is something else.
   This bond doth give thee here no jot of blood;
   The words expressly are 'a pound of flesh':
   Take then thy bond, take thou thy pound of flesh;   305
   But, in the cutting it, if thou dost shed
   One drop of Christian blood, thy lands and goods
   Are, by the laws of Venice, confiscate
   Unto the state of Venice.

Gratiano: O upright judge! Mark, Jew: O learned judge!   310

Shylock: Is that the law?

Portia: Thyself shall see the act;
   For, as thou urgest justice, be assur'd
   Thou shalt have justice more than thou desir'st.

Gratiano: O learned judge! Mark, Jew: a learned judge!

Shylock: I take this offer then: pay the bond thrice,   315
   And let the Christian go.

Bassanio: Here is the money.

Portia: Soft!
   The Jew shall have all justice; soft! no haste:—
   He shall have nothing but the penalty.

Gratiano: O Jew! an upright judge, a learned judge!   320

Portia: Therefore prepare thee to cut off the flesh.
   Shed thou no blood; nor cut thou less, nor more,
   But just a pound of flesh: if thou tak'st more,
   Or less, than a just pound, be it but so much
   As makes it light or heavy in the substance,   325
   Or the division of the twentieth part
   Of one poor scruple, nay, if the scale do turn
   But in the estimation of a hair,

331   *on the hip:* at a disadvantage, at my mercy. Compare
       Shylock's earlier threat (Act 1, Scene 3, line 42).

333   *principal:* original sum borrowed (3000 ducats)

342   *give him good of it:* help him to enjoy it

343   *question:* argue

345   *enacted:* decreed

346   *alien:* non-citizen. Even if Shylock were born in Venice, he
       would not be a Venetian citizen, for Jews were not granted
       citizenship in most states of medieval Europe.

349   *party:* person. Portia's use of legal jargon suggests that she
       may have memorized the appropriate law. *contrive:* plot

351   *privy coffer:* state treasury (originally, for the private use of
       the sovereign)

353   *'gainst all other voice:* regardless of any other opinion

355   *by manifest proceeding:* from the obvious events of the
       inquiry

358   *incurr'd:* run into

359   *rehears'd:* outlined, reviewed

365   *That:* so that, in order that

Thou diest, and all thy goods are confiscate.
Gratiano: A second Daniel, a Daniel, Jew!   330
   Now, infidel, I have you on the hip.
Portia: Why doth the Jew pause? take thy forfeiture.
Shylock: Give me my principal, and let me go.
Bassanio: I have it ready for thee; here it is.
Portia: He hath refus'd it in the open court: 335
   He shall have merely justice, and his bond.
Gratiano: A Daniel, still say I; a second Daniel!
   I thank thee, Jew, for teaching me that word.
Shylock: Shall I not have barely my principal?
Portia: Thou shalt have nothing but the forfeiture,   340
   To be so taken at thy peril, Jew.
Shylock: Why, then the devil give him good of it!
   I'll stay no longer question.
Portia: Tarry, Jew:
   The law hath yet another hold on you.
   It is enacted in the laws of Venice,   345
   If it be prov'd against an alien
   That by direct or indirect attempts
   He seek the life of any citizen,
   The party 'gainst the which he doth contrive
   Shall seize one half his goods; the other half   350
   Comes to the privy coffer of the state;
   And the offender's life lies in the mercy
   Of the duke only, 'gainst all other voice.
   In which predicament, I say, thou stand'st;
   For it appears by manifest proceeding,   355
   That indirectly, and directly too,
   Thou hast contriv'd against the very life
   Of the defendant; and thou hast incurr'd
   The danger formerly by me rehears'd.
   Down therefore and beg mercy of the duke.   360
Gratiano: Beg that thou may'st have leave to hang thyself—
   And yet, thy wealth being forfeit to the state,
   Thou hast not left the value of a cord;
   Therefore thou must be hang'd at the state's charge.
Duke: That thou shalt see the difference of our spirit,   365
   I pardon thee thy life before thou ask it.
   For half thy wealth, it is Antonio's;

368   *general state:* general use of the state

369   *humbleness:* (on Shylock's part); *drive unto:* reduce to

372   *prop:* supporting pillar or beam

376   *halter:* hangman's noose; *gratis:* free of interest

377   *So please:* if it pleases

378   *quit:* cancel

379   *so:* as long as, provided that

380   *in use:* in trust (to use as I see fit)

384   *presently:* immediately. Though Antonio's demand seems unmerciful and even unreasonable to a modern audience, earlier Christian audiences would have seen it as an act of charity. They would have believed that Shylock's conversion would save his soul from eternal damnation. This issue was treated comically in the earlier scene between Launcelot and Jessica (Act 3, Scene 5, lines 1–19).

386   *all he dies possess'd:* all he owns when he dies

388   *recant:* withdraw, retract

389   *late:* recently

391   *I am content:* (Does Shylock have any alternative?)

395   *god-fathers:* Christian parents select a pair of close friends or relatives to help them in the spiritual education of their children. These *godparents* begin to play their role at the ceremony of baptism. In the next line, Gratiano jokingly refers to the twelve *god-fathers* who make up the twelve-man jury in a court of law. Gratiano claims that, had he been the judge, his jury would have condemned Shylock to death.

397   *font:* the basin, usually of stone, that holds the holy water used in the ceremony of baptism (referring here to Shylock's conversion)

401   *meet:* necessary

402   *your leisure serves you not:* you cannot afford time for relaxation

403   *gratify:* show your gratitude toward, reward

404   *bound:* indebted

The other half comes to the general state,
    Which humbleness may drive unto a fine.
Portia: Ay, for the state; not for Antonio.   370
Shylock: Nay, take my life and all; pardon not that:
    You take my house, when you do take the prop
    That doth sustain my house; you take my life
    When you do take the means whereby I live.
Portia: What mercy can you render him, Antonio?   375
Gratiano: A halter gratis; nothing else, for God's sake!
Antonio: So please my lord the duke, and all the court,
    To quit the fine for one half of his goods,
    I am content so he will let me have
    The other half in use, to render it,   380
    Upon his death, unto the gentleman
    That lately stole his daughter.
    Two things provided more, that, for this favour,
    He presently become a Christian;
    The other, that he do record a gift,   385
    Here in the court, of all he dies possess'd,
    Unto his son Lorenzo and his daughter.
Duke: He shall do this, or else I do recant
    The pardon that I late pronounced here.
Portia: Art thou contented, Jew? what dost thou say?   390
Shylock: I am content.
Portia: Clerk, draw a deed of gift.
Shylock: I pray you give me leave to go from hence:
    I am not well. Send the deed after me,
    And I will sign it.
Duke: Get thee gone, but do it.
Gratiano: In christening shalt thou have two god-fathers;   395
    Had I been judge, thou shouldst have had ten more,
    To bring thee to the gallows, not to the font.
                                          [*Exit Shylock*]
Duke: Sir, I entreat you home with me to dinner.
Portia: I humbly do desire your Grace of pardon:
    I must away this night toward Padua,   400
    And it is meet I presently set forth.
Duke: I am sorry that your leisure serves you not.
    Antonio, gratify this gentleman,
    For, in my mind, you are much bound to him.

407   *in lieu whereof:* in return for which

409   *freely:* willingly; *cope:* match (give as an equivalent for)

415   *mercenary:* motivated by money

416   *know:* recognize

418   *of force:* it is necessary; *attempt you further:* try harder to persuade you

419   *tribute:* token of respect

421   *Not to . . . pardon me:* Not to refuse my request and to excuse my insistence.

422   *You press me far:* you are very insistent

423   *Give me . . . sake:* This line is probably spoken to Antonio, the next obviously to Bassanio.

430   *And now . . . to it:* And now I have made up my mind to have it.

431   *There's more . . . the value:* More than the cost of the ring itself is at stake.

432   *dearest:* most expensive. He will buy her the most expensive ring to replace the one she wants from him.

433   *by proclamation:* with a public announcement (that I will buy it)

434   *for this:* for this particular ring

435   *liberal in offers:* generous in making promises (not in keeping them)

441   *'scuse:* excuse

[*Exeunt Duke, Merchants, and Officers of the Court*]

Bassanio: Most worthy gentleman, I and my friend   405
  Have by your wisdom been this day acquitted
  Of grievous penalties, in lieu whereof,
  Three thousand ducats, due unto the Jew,
  We freely cope your courteous pains withal.

Antonio: And stand indebted, over and above,   410
  In love and service to you evermore.

Portia: He is well paid that is well satisfied,
  And I, delivering you, am satisfied,
  And therein do account myself well paid:
  My mind was never yet more mercenary.   415
  I pray you, know me when we meet again:
  I wish you well, and so I take my leave.

Bassanio: Dear sir, of force I must attempt you further:
  Take some remembrance of us as a tribute,
  Not as a fee. Grant me two things, I pray you,   420
  Not to deny me, and to pardon me.

Portia: You press me far, and therefore I will yield.
  Give me your gloves, I'll wear them for your sake;
  And (for your love) I'll take this ring from you.
  Do not draw back your hand; I'll take no more,   425
  And you in love shall not deny me this.

Bassanio: This ring, good sir? alas! it is a trifle.
  I will not shame myself to give you this.

Portia: I will have nothing else but only this;
  And now methinks I have a mind to it.   430

Bassanio: There's more depends on this than on the value.
  The dearest ring in Venice will I give you,
  And find it out by proclamation:
  Only for this, I pray you, pardon me.

Portia: I see, sir, you are liberal in offers: 435
  You taught me first to beg, and now methinks
  You teach me how a beggar should be answer'd.

Bassanio: Good sir, this ring was given me by my wife,
  And, when she put it on, she made me vow
  That I should neither sell, nor give nor lose it.   440

Portia: That 'scuse serves many men to save their gifts.
  And if your wife be not a mad-woman,
  And know how well I have deserv'd this ring,

444   *hold out enemy:* be angry with you

448   *'gainst:* more highly than

452   *you and I will thither:* we will go there

She would not hold out enemy for ever,
For giving it to me. Well, peace be with you.   445
       [*Exeunt Portia and Nerissa*]
Antonio: My Lord Bassanio, let him have the ring:
 Let his deservings and my love withal
 Be valu'd 'gainst your wife's commandement.
Bassanio: Go, Gratiano; run and overtake him;
 Give him the ring, and bring him, if thou canst,   450
 Unto Antonio's house. Away, make haste.
         [*Exit Gratiano*]
 Come, you and I will thither presently,
 And in the morning early will we both
 Fly toward Belmont. Come, Antonio.   [*Exeunt*]

1   *this deed:* the deed of gift arranged in the previous scene (Act 4, Scene 1, line 393)

5   *o'erta'en:* overtaken

6   *upon more advice:* after further consideration

15   *I warrant:* I guarantee; *old:* abundant

17   *outface:* outdo them in insisting (What, then, does *outswear* mean?)

Scene 2

Venice. A street.
Enter Portia and Nerissa.

Portia: Inquire the Jew's house out, give him this deed,
  And let him sign it. We'll away tonight,
  And be a day before our husbands home:
  This deed will be well welcome to Lorenzo.
  [*Enter Gratiano*]
Gratiano: Fair sir, you are well o'erta'en.   5
  My Lord Bassanio, upon more advice,
  Hath sent you here this ring, and doth entreat
  Your company at dinner.
Portia: That cannot be.
  His ring I do accept most thankfully,
  And so, I pray you, tell him: furthermore,   10
  I pray you, show my youth old Shylock's house.
Gratiano: That will I do.
Nerissa: Sir, I would speak with you.
  [*Aside to Portia*] I'll see if I can get my husband's ring.
  Which I did make him swear to keep for ever.
Portia: Thou may'st, I warrant. We shall have old swearing   15
  That they did give the rings away to men;
  But we'll outface them, and outswear them too.
  Away, make haste! thou know'st where I will tarry.
Nerissa: Come, good sir, will you show me to this house?
                                         [*Exeunt*]

Act 4, Scenes 1 and 2: Activities

1. So can I give no reason, nor I will not,
   More than a lodg'd hate and a certain loathing
   I bear Antonio . . . (Scene 1, lines 59–61)

   Earlier in the play, Shylock has outlined his complaints
   against Antonio: once to himself (Act 1, Scene 3, lines
   37–48) and once under great emotional stress (Act 3,
   Scene 1, lines 48–67). Why do you think he does not
   explain his reasons when asked in open court? Record
   your first thoughts in your journal. Then, compare notes
   and discuss your opinions with a partner.

2. Reread Antonio's speech beginning, "I pray you, think you
   question with the Jew . . ." (Scene 1, lines 70–83). How do
   the images Antonio uses confirm our impression of his
   prejudice? What effect would this speech have upon
   Shylock? Does it affect your opinion of Antonio? How does
   your opinion of him change by the end of the scene and
   why? Record your answers in your notebook.

3. Early in Scene 1, Shylock claims that Antonio's pound of
   flesh has been "dearly bought" (line 100). In a small
   group, make a list of all the "payments" you think Shylock
   has made for the pound of flesh.

4. At this point, both Shylock and Antonio are locked into
   positions. By going to trial, one of them will win; the other
   will lose everything. Imagine that they were not in a
   courtroom but instead were sitting together to negotiate a
   solution that would satisfy both of them, and that you were
   their mediator.

   Skillful negotiators know how important it is to separate
   your *position* (what you demand) from your *interest* (what
   you really want). Positions can be altered with careful
   negotiation, but interests do not change.

   a) What would you say are the true interests of both
      Shylock and Antonio? As the mediator, how would you
      help each of them to express their true interests? Role-
      play this scene in a trio with one of you playing yourself
      as the mediator.

Assuming that the true interests are "on the table," what solutions would you offer that might satisfy both of them without the need for a trial? Continue the role-play and see if you can bring it to a "win/win" conclusion. Remember, those playing Shylock and Antonio may change their positions but must insist that their interests are satisfied.

b) From a dramatic perspective, why would Shakespeare have chosen a trial over a negotiated settlement? Discuss your answers within your group.

5. Portia's speech on the "quality of mercy" (lines 181–202) is based upon the Christian belief that, since no one is free of sin, everyone requires God's mercy to be saved from eternal damnation. In other words, no one is perfect, but we can aspire to godliness through "God-like" acts of mercy. Shylock misunderstands: he has done nothing illegal, and so, he feels, he has no need of mercy.

If you could stop the hearing and talk to Shylock, what would you say to help him understand Portia's speech more fully?

a) Record your preparatory notes in your journal.

b) In small groups, discuss the meaning of Portia's speech in order to clarify and organize your thoughts. Then, compare your notes.

c) Share your advice to Shylock with the class.

6. "To do a great right, do a little wrong . . ." (line 213)

As a class activity, discuss what "little wrong" Bassanio suggests. In your discussion, consider the following questions: In what situations, if any, might you advise "doing a little wrong" in order to achieve a greater good? Would you lie to protect a friend? Would you steal to feed a starving child? Why does Portia reject Bassanio's argument? Do you agree with her reasoning or with Bassanio's?

7. Conduct a debate: Be it resolved that, in the courtroom scene, Bassanio finally shows qualities and values that make him deserving of Portia's love.

8. Portia's judgment that "This bond doth give thee here no jot of blood" (line 303) marks a turning point in the courtroom scene. Shylock is given very little opportunity to express in words his reaction to this turn of events. Clearly, the actor who plays Shylock has to convey his changing responses through actions.

In a director's log, make notes to describe what emotions you expect the actor to show from the turning point of this scene to its conclusion. Use the few lines of speech that Shylock does have as a guide. Note also the final impression of Shylock that the actor should convey to the audience. Create or find a piece of art that conveys to you Shylock's emotional response to the outcome of the trial.

9. "Love thy neighbour as thyself." (*Matthew* 22:39)

As a rabbi, Jesus reminded his fellow Jews of the critical importance of charity to their religion.

Though Shylock himself is too damaged by pain, resentment, and anger to remember the message, toward the end of the hearing, Antonio and the Duke both display the spirit of charity prescribed in Jesus' commandment.

a) In your notebook, outline the acts of mercy that Antonio and the Duke show Shylock (lines 365–389). Be sure to consider the exact terms of Shylock's sentence. Investigate why Shylock's forced conversion to Christianity would have been considered an act of mercy in Shakespeare's time.

b) In a small group, assess the fairness of Shylock's sentence in a modern context. What historical examples of forced conversions have affected our attitudes toward this practice?

c) How would this sentence stand up in an International Court of Justice? (Consider the tenets of the Universal Declaration of Human Rights, which you can easily find on the Internet at www.un.org/overview/rights.html.)

10. You are a lawyer representing either Shylock or Antonio at this courtroom hearing. Use the Internet to find out about typical legal objections. Using what you have learned,

identify those statements and actions throughout the hearing to which you would object on behalf of your client. In each case, state the grounds of your objection.

In groups of three, act out short sections of the hearing. Two lawyers should insert objections on behalf of their clients, Antonio and Shylock, and the judge should sustain or overrule the objections.

11. a) In pairs, prepare and make an audio or video recording of a news interview with Portia/Balthazar after the court hearing. Plan your questions carefully in advance, designing them to cover the range of your viewers' or listeners' interests. Be sure to find out why Portia put Antonio through so much anxiety before revealing the legal argument that she knew would foil Shylock's plan.

b) Conduct a similar interview with Antonio. Your viewers or listeners will have a wide range of questions for him as well. In particular, they will want to know about his thoughts at the point of death, his relief at his escape, and his decision to be merciful to the enemy who had just tried to kill him.

c) On your own, use these interviews to prepare a feature article on the hearing for a newspaper or newsmagazine.

12. What reasons might Shakespeare have had for including the device of the "ring plot" immediately following the courtroom scene? As Shakespeare, record your reasons in a journal entry.

For the next scene . . .

In some ways the story of the play is over. But what "loose ends" need to be tied up in order for the play to have a satisfying conclusion for you?

Act 5, Scene 1

In this scene . . .

Lorenzo and Jessica wander in the moonlit gardens of
Belmont. They compare themselves to other pairs of
famous lovers and comment on the soothing power of
beautiful music. Portia and Nerissa arrive home from
Venice, just before their husbands return to Belmont.

Before long, Portia and Nerissa steer the
conversation to the topic of the wedding rings, and a
heated argument begins when Bassanio and Gratiano
admit that they have given their rings away. After much
teasing, Portia reveals the true identities of Balthazar
and his clerk. She adds to the merriment by announcing
that three of Antonio's ships have returned safely and by
presenting Jessica and Lorenzo with the contract by
which they will inherit Shylock's wealth. In a mood of
celebration, Antonio and the three pairs of happy lovers
leave the stage.

211

4   *Troilus:* During the Trojan War, young Troilus was separated from Cressida when she was taken hostage and carried off to the Greek encampment. The pair vowed to be faithful to one another, and Troilus became a symbol of the faithful lover.

7   *Thisbe:* The love between Pyramus and Thisbe was forbidden by their parents. They planned to meet by moonlight in the woods. Arriving first, Thisbe was frightened by a lion and sought safety in a nearby cave. The lion mauled the scarf that she had dropped in her panic. Finding the scarf, Pyramus assumed Thisbe had been killed and stabbed himself. In her grief, Thisbe took her own life. *o'ertrip:* step lightly over, dance over

8   *ere himself:* before she saw the lion

10   *Dido:* the queen of Carthage who was deserted by her lover Aeneas when his sense of duty compelled him to set sail for Italy; *willow:* The willow tree is symbolic of forsaken love.

11   *waft:* waved to

13   *Medea:* the young princess who fled from Colchis with Jason and the golden fleece. Later, she used her magical powers to rejuvenate Jason's father, Aeson.

15   *steal:* (What is the pun?)

16   *unthrift love:* penniless lover (Lorenzo). Lorenzo might also be joking about Jessica's unwise affection for him.

19   *Stealing:* taking possession of

21   *shrew:* a scolding, bad-tempered woman

23   *out-night:* Jessica invents the verb for this occasion. (What does she mean? Compare *outface* and *outswear* in Act 4, Scene 2, line 17.)

Act 5, Scene 1

*Belmont. The garden in front of
Portia's house.*

Enter Lorenzo and Jessica.

Lorenzo: The moon shines bright: in such a night as this,
When the sweet wind did gently kiss the trees,
And they did make no noise, in such a night
Troilus methinks mounted the Trojan walls,
And sigh'd his soul toward the Grecian tents,   5
Where Cressid lay that night.
Jessica: In such a night
Did Thisbe fearfully o'ertrip the dew,
And saw the lion's shadow ere himself,
And ran dismay'd away.
Lorenzo: In such a night
Stood Dido with a willow in her hand   10
Upon the wild sea-banks, and waft her love
To come again to Cathage.
Jessica: In such a night
Medea gather'd the enchanted herbs
That did renew old Æson.
Lorenzo: In such a night
Did Jessica steal from the wealthy Jew,   15
And with an unthrift love did run from Venice,
As far as Belmont.
Jessica: In such a night
Did young Lorenzo swear he lov'd her well,
Stealing her soul with many vows of faith,
And ne'er a true one.   20
Lorenzo: In such a night
Did pretty Jessica, like a little shrew,
Slander her love, and he forgave it her.
Jessica: I would out-night you, did nobody come;

24   *footing:* footsteps

31   *holy crosses:* small roadside shrines where travellers could
      pray

39   *Sola . . . sola!:* Launcelot imitates the sound of a post horn
      or bugle. *Sola* seems to be a combination of *soh* and *lah*,
      two of the eight notes on the musical scale. The *wo ha, ho!*
      addresses his make-believe horse and commands it to stop.

43   *Leave hollowing:* stop shouting

46   *post:* messenger

49   *expect:* await

51   *signify:* announce

57   *Become:* suit

59   *patens:* small discs of shiny metal (that is, the stars)

But, hark! I hear the footing of a man.
[*Enter Stephano*]
Lorenzo: Who comes so fast in silence of the night?   25
Stephano: A friend.
Lorenzo: A friend! what friend? your name, I pray you,
       friend.
Stephano: Stephano is my name; and I bring word
       My mistress will before the break of day
       Be here at Belmont: she doth stray about   30
       By holy crosses, where she kneels and prays
       For happy wedlock hours.
Lorenzo: Who comes with her?
Stephano: None but a holy hermit and her maid.
       I pray you, is my master yet return'd?
Lorenzo: He is not, nor we have not heard from him.   35
       But go we in, I pray thee, Jessica,
       And ceremoniously let us prepare
       Some welcome for the mistress of the house.
       [*Enter Launcelot*]
Launcelot: Sola, sola! wo ha, ho! sola, sola!
Lorenzo: Who calls?   40
Launcelot: Sola! did you see Master Lorenzo? Master
       Lorenzo! sola, sola!
Lorenzo: Leave hollowing, man; here.
Launcelot: Sola! where? where?
Lorenzo: Here.   45
Launcelot: Tell him there's a post come from my master,
       with his horn full of good news: my master will be here
       ere morning.   [*Exit*]
Lorenzo: Sweet soul, let's in, and there expect their coming.
       And yet no matter; why should we go in?   50
       My friend Stephano, signify, I pray you,
       Within the house, your mistress is at hand;
       And bring your music forth into the air.   [*Exit Stephano*]
       How sweet the moonlight sleeps upon this bank!
       Here will we sit, and let the sounds of music   55
       Creep in our ears: soft stillness and the night
       Become the touches of sweet harmony.
       Sit, Jessica—look how the floor of heaven
       Is thick inlaid with patens of bright gold:

60	*orb:* sphere (that is, a star or planet)
60-65	*There's not . . . hear it:* The Elizabethans believed that, as the stars and the planets moved through the heavens, they created musical harmony. However, as Lorenzo explains, we cannot hear this music as long as the soul is trapped in the body.
61	*his motion:* its movement
62	*Still quiring:* forever singing in perfect harmony; *young-eyed cherubins:* bright-eyed angels
64	*muddy vesture of decay:* clothing of mortality (that is, the body)
65	*grossly:* roughly, coarsely
66	*Diana:* the classical goddess of the moon. Each evening, she comes down from heaven to sleep with her mortal lover, Endymion (line 109).
69	*I am never . . . sweet music:* Jessica notes that listening to music makes her solemn and philosophical.
71	*wanton:* frisky
72	*race:* small group; *unhandled:* unbroken
73	*Fetching mad bounds:* leaping about wildly
74	*condition:* nature
75	*perchance:* perhaps
76	*air:* melody
77	*make a mutual stand:* all stand still together
78	*modest:* gentle, calm
79	*the poet:* The Latin poet Ovid told the story of Orpheus, whose music could draw lifeless objects to his side; he was also able to tame wild beasts.
80	*feign:* imagine
81	*Since naught so stockish:* for (there is) nothing so dull or stupid
84	*concord:* harmony
85	*stratagems:* plots, acts of deceit, deceptions; *spoils:* destruction
87	*affections:* personality; *Erebus:* the personification of darkness in classical mythology (the son of Chaos and brother of Night)
88	*Mark:* pay attention to
91	*naughty:* wicked
94	*substitute:* deputy, viceroy
95-96	*his state Empties itself:* his glory immediately disappears

There's not the smallest orb which thou behold'st   60
But in his motion like an angel sings,
Still quiring to the young-eyed cherubins;
Such harmony is in immortal souls,
But whilst this muddy vesture of decay
Doth grossly close it in, we cannot hear it.   65
[*Enter Musicians*]
Come, ho! and wake Diana with a hymn:
With sweetest touches pierce your mistress' ear,
And draw her home with music.   [*Music*]
Jessica: I am never merry when I hear sweet music.
Lorenzo: The reason is, your spirits are attentive: 70
For do but note a wild and wanton herd,
Or race of youthful and unhandled colts,
Fetching mad bounds, bellowing and neighing loud,
Which is the hot condition of their blood;
If they but hear perchance a trumpet sound,   75
Or any air of music touch their ears,
You shall perceive them make a mutual stand,
Their savage eyes turn'd to a modest gaze
By the sweet power of music: therefore the poet
Did feign that Orpheus drew trees, stones, and floods;   80
Since naught so stockish, hard, and full of rage,
But music for the time doth change his nature.
The man that hath no music in himself,
Nor is not mov'd with concord of sweet sounds,
Is fit for treasons, stratagems, and spoils;   85
The motions of his spirit are dull as night,
And his affections dark as Erebus:
Let no such man be trusted. Mark the music.
[*Enter Portia and Nerissa*]
Portia: That light we see is burning in my hall.
How far that little candle throws his beams!   90
So shines a good deed in a naughty world.
Nerissa: When the moon shone, we did not see the candle.
Portia: So doth the greater glory dim the less:
A substitute shines brightly as a king
Until a king be by, and then his state   95
Empties itself, as doth an inland brook
Into the main of waters, Music! hark!

98   *your music . . . of the house:* As we saw in Act 3, Portia employs a small band of musicians as part of her household staff.

99   *Nothing . . . without respect:* Our judgments vary according to circumstances.

103   *When neither is attended:* when each is alone

104   *The nightingale . . . by day:* The nightingale was thought to sing only at night (when all other songbirds were asleep and silent).

107   *season:* good timing; *season'd:* improved

108   *right praise:* true value

115   *Which speed . . . the better for:* who benefit because of

119-120 *take No note:* say nothing

123   *tell-tales:* tellers of secrets

127   *Antipodes:* those people who live on the other side of the world

127-128 *We should hold . . . of the sun:* Bassanio's compliment corresponds roughly to our modern-day folksong "You Are My Sunshine."

129   *light:* flighty, unfaithful

130   *heavy:* sad

Nerissa: It is your music, madam, of the house.
Portia: Nothing is good, I see, without respect:
   Methinks it sounds much sweeter than by day. 100
Nerissa: Silence bestows that virtue on it, madam.
Portia: The crow doth sing as sweetly as the lark
   When neither is attended, and I think
   The nightingale, if she should sing by day
   When every goose is cackling, would be thought 105
   No better a musician than the wren.
   How many things by season season'd are
   To their right praise and true perfection!
   Peace, ho! the moon sleeps with Endymion,
   And would not be awak'd!   [*Music ceases*] 110
Lorenzo: That is the voice,
   Or I am much deceiv'd, of Portia.
Portia: He knows me, as the blind man knows the cuckoo,
   By the bad voice.
Lorenzo: Dear lady, welcome home.
Portia: We have been praying for our husbands' welfare,
   Which speed, we hope, the better for our words. 115
   Are they return'd?
Lorenzo: Madam, they are not yet;
   But there is come a messenger before,
   To signify their coming.
Portia: Go in, Nerissa:
   Give order to my servants that they take
   No note at all of our being absent hence; 120
   Nor you, Lorenzo; Jessica, nor you.
                  [*A trumpet sounds*]
Lorenzo: Your husband is at hand, I hear his trumpet;
   We are no tell-tales, madam, fear you not.
Portia: This night methinks is but the daylight sick;
   It looks a little paler: 'tis a day, 125
   Such as the day is when the sun is hid.
   [*Enter Bassanio, Antonio, Gratiano, and their Servants*]
Bassanio: We should hold day with the Antipodes,
   If you would walk in absence of the sun.
Portia: Let me give light, but let me not be light;
   For a light wife doth make a heavy husband, 130
   And never be Bassanio so for me:

132   *God sort all!:* Let God make all the decisions!

135   *bound:* indebted

138   *acquitted of:* released from

141   *scant:* cut short; *breathing courtesy:* polite conversation ("small talk")

144   *Would he were gelt:* I wish he had been castrated; *for my part:* as far as I'm concerned
145   *at heart:* to heart
147   *paltry:* worthless
148   *posy:* sentimental phrase or verse engraved on a ring
149   *cutler's poetry:* Cutlers, or knife-makers, sometimes inscribed short verses on their knife handles.
151   *What:* Why?

156   *respective:* careful

158   *on's:* on his
159   *and if:* if ever

162   *scrubbed:* stunted, short

164   *prating:* chattering

But God sort all! You are welcome home, my lord.
Bassanio: I thank you, madam. Give welcome to my friend:
    This is the man, this is Antonio,
    To whom I am so infinitely bound.   135
Portia: You should in all sense be much bound to him,
    For, as I hear, he was much bound for you.
Antonio: No more than I am well acquitted of.
Portia: Sir, you are very welcome to our house:
    It must appear in other ways than words,   140
    Therefore I scant this breathing courtesy.
Gratiano: [*To Nerissa*] By yonder moon I swear you do me
      wrong;
    In faith, I give it to the judge's clerk;
    Would he were gelt that had it, for my part,
    Since you do take it, love, so much at heart.   145
Portia: A quarrel, ho, already! what's the matter?
Gratiano: About a hoop of gold, a paltry ring
    That she did give me, whose posy was
    For all the world like cutler's poetry
    Upon a knife, 'Love me, and leave me not'.   150
Nerissa: What talk you of the posy, or the value?
    You swore to me, when I did give it you,
    That you would wear it till your hour of death,
    And that it should lie with you in your grave:
    Though not for me, yet for your vehement oaths,   155
    You should have been respective and have kept it.
    Gave it a judge's clerk! no, God's my judge,
    The clerk will ne'er wear hair on's face that had it.
Gratiano: He will, and if he live to be a man.
Nerissa: Ay, if a woman live to be a man.   160
Gratiano: Now, by this hand, I gave it to a youth,
    A kind of boy, a little scrubbed boy,
    No higher than thyself, the judge's clerk.
    A prating boy that begg'd it as a fee:
    I could not for my heart deny it him.   165
Portia: You were to blame—I must be plain with you—
    To part so slightly with your wife's first gift;
    A thing stuck on with oaths upon your finger,
    And so riveted with faith unto your flesh.
    I gave my love a ring and made him swear   170

172   *leave:* part with

174   *masters:* possesses

176   *And 'twere to me:* if it had been done to me

198   *abate:* lessen
199   *virtue:* power

201   *contain:* keep, look after

205   *terms of zeal:* determination
205-206 *wanted the modesty . . . ceremony:* that he could have been so bad-mannered as to insist on having something that was so important to you

Never to part with it: and here he stands;
I dare be sworn for him he would not leave it,
Not pluck it from his finger, for the wealth
That the world masters. Now, in faith, Gratiano,
You give your wife too unkind a cause of grief: 175
And 'twere to me, I should be mad at it.
Bassanio: [*Aside*] Why, I were best to cut my left hand off,
And swear I lost the ring defending it.
Gratiano: My Lord Bassanio gave his ring away
Unto the judge that begg'd it, and indeed   180
Deserv'd it too; and then the boy, his clerk,
That took some pains in writing, he begg'd mine;
And neither man nor master would take aught
But the two rings.
Portia: What ring gave you, my lord?
Not that, I hope, which you receiv'd of me.   185
Bassanio: If I could add a lie unto a fault,
I would deny it; but you see my finger
Hath not the ring upon it—it is gone.
Portia: Even so void is your false heart of truth.
By heaven, I will ne're come in your bed   190
Until I see the ring.
Nerissa: Nor I in yours,
Till I again see mine.
Bassanio: Sweet Portia,
If you did know to whom I gave the ring,
If you did know for whom I gave the ring,
And would conceive for what I gave the ring,   195
And how unwillingly I left the ring,
When naught would be accepted but the ring,
You would abate the strength of your displeasure.
Portia: If you had known the virtue of the ring,
Or half her worthiness that gave the ring,   200
Or your own honour to contain the ring,
You would not then have parted with the ring.
What man is there so much unreasonable,
If you had pleas'd to have defended it
With any terms of zeal, wanted the modesty   205
To urge the thing held as a ceremony?
Nerissa teaches me what to believe:

208	*I'll die for 't:* I'm sure. (Notice how Portia's mock anger moves her to hyperbole.)
210	*civil doctor:* both a doctor of *civil law* and a *well-bred* doctor
213	*suffer'd:* allowed
214	*held up:* saved (that is, argued for)
217	*beset:* overcome
219	*besmear:* stain (my honour)
220	*blessed candles of the night:* the stars
226	*liberal:* free in giving
229	*Know:* Shakespeare's audience would interpret this verb in a sexual sense. (Compare this line to Portia's promise in Act 4, Scene 1, line 416.)
230	*Argus:* in classical mythology, a creature with a hundred eyes. Juno hired him to keep jealous watch over one of her unfaithful husband's lovers.
234	*be well advis'd:* be careful
235	*to mine own protection:* to guard my own honour
236	*take:* catch
237	*mar:* damage
239	*notwithstanding:* nonetheless
240	*this enforced wrong:* this crime that was forced upon me

I'll die for 't, but some woman had the ring.
Bassanio: No, by my honour, madam, by my soul,
    No woman had it, but a civil doctor, 210
    Which did refuse three thousand ducats of me,
    And begg'd the ring, the which I did deny him,
    And suffer'd him to go displeas'd away;
    Even he that had held up the very life
    Of my dear friend. What should I say, sweet lady? 215
    I was enforc'd to send it after him.
    I was beset with shame and courtesy;
    My honour would not let ingratitude
    So much besmear it. Pardon me, good lady,
    For by these blessed candles of the night, 220
    Had you been there, I think you would have begg'd
    The ring of me to give the worthy doctor.
Portia: Let not that doctor e'er come near my house.
    Since he hath got the jewel that I lov'd,
    And that which you did swear to keep for me; 225
    I will become as liberal as you—
    I'll not deny him anything I have,
    No, not my body, nor my husband's bed.
    Know him I shall, I am well sure of it.
    Lie not a night from home; watch me like Argus: 230
    If you do not, if I be left alone,
    Now by mine honour, which is yet mine own,
    I'll have that doctor for my bedfellow.
Nerissa: And I his clerk; therefore be well advis'd
    How you do leave me to mine own protection. 235
Gratiano: Well, do you so: let not me take him, then,
    For if I do, I'll mar the young clerk's pen.
Antonio: I am th' unhappy subject of these quarrels.
Portia: Sir, grieve not you; you are welcome notwith-
    standing.
Bassanio: Portia, forgive me this enforced wrong; 240
    And in the hearing of these many friends,
    I swear to thee, even by thine own fair eyes,
    Wherein I see myself—
Portia: Mark you but that!
    In both my eyes he doubly sees himself;
    In each eye, one: swear by your double self, 245

246   *oath of credit:* believable promise (not believable, of course, at all if Portia's *double* means deceitful)

249   *wealth:* well-being, welfare

251   *Had . . . miscarried:* would have been lost

253   *advisedly:* deliberately
254   *surety:* guarantee

262   *In lieu of:* in return for
263-264 *this is like . . . fair enough:* A new wife should not need a lover when her young husband is still lusty and amorous. Her taking of a lover is like repairing roads in summer— completely unnecessary.
265   *cuckolds:* men whose wives are unfaithful
266   *grossly:* indecently, coarsely; *amaz'd:* confused, befuddled

277   *Are richly come:* have arrived with rich cargo; *suddenly:* unexpectedly

279   *dumb:* speechless

And there's an oath of credit.
Bassanio: Nay, but hear me:
   Pardon this fault, and by my soul I swear
   I never more will break an oath with thee.
Antonio: I once did lend my body for his wealth,
   Which, but for him that had your husband's ring,   250
   Had quite miscarried: I dare be bound again,
   My soul upon the forfeit, that your lord
   Will never more break faith advisedly.
Portia: Then you shall be his surety. Give him this,
   And bid him keep it better than the other.   255
Antonio: Here, Lord Bassanio; swear to keep this ring.
Bassanio: By heaven! it is the same I gave the doctor!
Portia: I had it of him: pardon me, Bassanio,
   For, by this ring, the doctor lay with me.
Nerissa: And pardon me, my gentle Gratiano;   260
   For that same scrubbed boy, the doctor's clerk,
   In lieu of this, last night did lie with me.
Gratiano: Why, this is like the mending of highways
   In summer, where the ways are fair enough!
   What, are we cuckolds ere we have deserv'd it?   265
Portia: Speak not so grossly. You are all amaz'd:
   Here is a letter, read it at your leisure,
   It comes from Padua, from Bellario:
   There you shall find that Portia was the doctor,
   Nerissa there her clerk. Lorenzo here   270
   Shall witness I set forth as soon as you,
   And even but now return'd; I have not yet
   Enter'd my house. Antonio, you are welcome;
   And I have better news in store for you
   Than you expect: unseal this letter soon;   275
   There you shall find three of your argosies
   Are richly come to harbour suddenly.
   You shall not know by what strange accident
   I chanced on this letter.
Antonio: I am dumb.
Bassanio: Were you the doctor, and I knew you not?   280
Gratiano: Were you the clerk that is to make me cuckold?
Nerissa: Ay, but the clerk that never means to do it,
   Unless he live until he be a man.

288   *road:* anchorage (see note on Act 1, Scene 1, line 19)

294   *manna:* the miraculous food that fell from the sky for the Israelites as they were starving in the wilderness on their journey from Egypt to the promised land (*Exodus* 16:15). Lorenzo uses the allusion to mean unexpected fortune.

297   *at full:* in detail

298   *charge us . . . inter'gatories:* In court, witnesses were called upon to answer under oath a series of questions (*interrogatories*).

305   *That:* so that; *couching:* going to bed (from the French, *coucher*)

307   *sore:* sorely, greatly, highly

Bassanio: Sweet doctor, you shall be my bedfellow:
   When I am absent, then lie with my wife. 285
Antonio: Sweet lady, you have given me life and living;
   For here I read for certain that my ships
   Are safely come to road.
Portia: How now, Lorenzo!
   My clerk hath some good comforts too for you.
Nerissa: Ay, and I'll give them him without a fee. 290
   There do I give to you and Jessica,
   From the rich Jew, a special deed of gift,
   After his death, of all he dies possess'd of.
Lorenzo: Fair ladies, you drop manna in the way
   Of starved people. 295
Portia: It is almost morning,
   And yet I am sure you are not satisfied
   Of these events at full. Let us go in;
   And charge us there upon inter'gatories,
   And we will answer all things faithfully.
Gratiano: Let it be so: the first inter'gatory 300
   That my Nerissa shall be sworn on is,
   Whether till the next night she had rather stay,
   Or go to bed now, being two hours to day:
   But were the day come, I should wish it dark,
   That I were couching with the doctor's clerk. 305
   Well, while I live, I'll fear no other thing
   So sore as keeping safe Nerissa's ring.   *[Exeunt]*

Act 5, Scene 1: Activities

1. This scene begins with a spirited contest in which Lorenzo and Jessica compete to "out-night" each other with a series of allusions to famous lovers in classical literature.

   With a partner, make a list of other pairs of lovers whose stories they might have used in their competition. For the story of each pair, identify the event that best suggests the romantic atmosphere of the nighttime setting in Lorenzo's and Jessica's stories. You may need to embellish some of the stories with original incidents and details to achieve this. Be sure to include a variety of mythological, historical, and contemporary pairs. Romeo and Juliet, Orpheus and Eurydice, Samson and Delilah, Frankie and Johnny, Antony and Cleopatra, and the Duke and Duchess of Windsor are some examples.

   On your own, try extending the "out-nighting" dialogue between Lorenzo and Jessica, using your best examples. If you enjoy the challenge of writing verse, try to follow the metrical pattern established in the dialogue. Or you could create a board game that tests players' knowledge of the famous lovers' stories, and test your game out on your peers.

2. Assume you are the musical director of a production of *The Merchant of Venice* and you have to choose music to accompany lines 54–110 of this scene. What music would you choose? With a partner, select a portion of these lines to read to the class with the music you have chosen in the background. Or, you may choose to record the lines and the music, and play it for the class. With the class, discuss the appropriateness and effectiveness of your choices.

3. Much of the humour in the dialogue about the rings comes not from the lines alone, but from the looks, the gestures, and the vocal inflections that would be used by the actors.

   In groups of four or five, reread lines 142–237. Discuss fully the ways in which you could maximize the humour in playing the scene. Select a portion of the scene for rehearsal and presentation to the class.

4. Shakespeare does not explain how Antonio's ships have been saved or why they were missing for so long. Imagine that the letter Portia delivers is from Antonio's business manager in Venice. Write the letter, explaining why there has been such a serious misunderstanding, and how Antonio's three ships were saved.

5. a) The play ends on a note of harmony and celebration as Antonio and the three loving couples laugh and joke together. Will the characters all live "happily ever after," as in a fairy tale? Discuss your ideas with a small group.

   b) Assume that, as Shakespeare, you want to write a sequel to this play, set five years later. Prepare brief notes to describe the circumstances of the main characters at the start of your new play. How have their lives changed now that the celebrations of *The Merchant of Venice* have faded into memory? For instance, has Bassanio wasted all of Portia's wealth? Has Antonio succeeded in business, or has he suffered through more risky business ventures? How have Nerissa and Gratiano settled into married life? How are Jessica and Lorenzo supporting themselves until they can inherit Shylock's money? How has Shylock adapted to life as a Christian? Have he and Jessica been reconciled?

   Summarize your notes and compare them with summaries prepared by classmates.

Consider the Whole Play

1. Now that you have finished your reading of *The Merchant of Venice*, you will probably want to discuss, in small groups or as a class, some of the issues and concerns on which the play is built. Some of the main questions include:

   • What are the values and responsibilities of friendship?

   • What is "true love"?

   • Why are we so often "deceiv'd with ornament" (Act 3, Scene 2, line 74)?

   • What are the obligations of children to parents, and parents to children?

   • When is a risk worth taking?

   • Can there be justice without mercy?

   • Are there rules or laws that should be broken?

   In your discussion, consider how your understanding of the play and your personal experience led you to your conclusions.

   Choose one of the above topics, and prepare a short personal essay in which you explore the relevance of the theme in your own life.

   OR

   Prepare a literary essay in which you explore Shakespeare's treatment of one of these topics in the context of this play. Be sure to support your conclusions with direct references to the text.

2. *The Merchant of Venice* is a play about which there are many opposing views. Consider all of the following topics and choose one for formal classroom debate. Prepare your argument and be ready to defend it in the context of your knowledge of the whole play.

   a) Shylock's famous speech, "Hath not a Jew eyes?" (Act 3, Scene 1, line 53), is a cold-blooded justification of revenge, not a plea for tolerance.

b) The world is still "deceiv'd with ornament" (Act 3, Scene 2, line 74).

c) Bassanio is a superficial fool.

d) Money is more important than friendship.

e) Obedience to parents is a child's prime obligation.

f) Nothing can be gained without risk.

g) It is impossible for a modern audience to enjoy *The Merchant of Venice* because of the play's prejudice.

Alternatively, you may choose to defend your point of view in writing.

3. Many teenagers identify with Shylock's predicament more easily than adults and, consequently, share a common bond with him. Perhaps the fact that many teens feel themselves to be persecuted or "outsiders" provides one explanation for this attachment.

In small groups, discuss the validity of this observation. Consider carefully your own reaction to Shylock and his predicament and the reactions of your classmates. Do you identify at all with Shylock? Do you think that your situation resembles his in any way?

Organize your own thoughts and feelings in a personal essay, or use your ideas as the basis for a short story or poem about a contemporary teen in a similar situation.

4. As a class, publish a newspaper that might appear in Venice on the day after the trial. You will need to divide yourselves into "sections": world news, local news, editorial page, sports, "society" page, want ads, and others you may choose, with section editors reporting to the editor-in-chief.

Section editors should assign stories to each group member. Stories may be researched and written independently or in pairs. Reporters submit copy to their section editors for proofreading; revised copy is then submitted to the editor-in-chief for consideration.

A meeting of all editors will be needed to make final editorial decisions and to determine the layout of the paper.

You might need assistance in having the paper duplicated; perhaps you could arrange to have copies made at a print shop.

Have fun!

5. A knowledge of the importance of Venice during the Renaissance greatly enhances our appreciation of the society presented in *The Merchant of Venice*.

    Find out all you can about medieval Venice. In your research, you might consider some of the following topics:

    - the advantages of Venice's geographical position

    - the goods most often traded in Venice

    - the cosmopolitan character of the city

    - the architectural and artistic splendour of the city

    - the establishment of banks

    - the way the city was governed

    Two books you might find helpful are:

    McNeill, W.H: *Venice: The Hinge of Europe*
    Morris, Jan: *The Venetian Empire: A Sea Voyage*

    a) Create a presentation that will involve your classmates in the experience of Venice. Take full advantage of the wealth of visual material available (slides, postcards, maps, travel brochures, digital images), and use your imagination to bring Venice to your classroom.

    b) Create an advertising poster for a modern interpretation of *The Merchant of Venice*. Complete the project using a large-style format (poster board) and found or created images. Choose your symbols carefully so that the potential audience will not only notice, but be intrigued by the play you are promoting.

6. Portia, Nerissa, and Jessica all appear in *The Merchant of Venice* disguised as young men. *Twelfth Night* and *As You Like It* are two other Shakespearean comedies that have heroines in male disguise. Many other works of fiction also have included heroines disguised as males.

With the help of your teacher or librarian, locate and read one of these works to discover the reason for the disguise, the troubles and conflicts the disguise causes, and the contribution it makes to the final outcome. Present your findings to the class.

7. *The Merchant of Venice* contains many lines and images that stimulate creative thought. Use one of the following quotations as a springboard for creative writing. Before you begin, decide on a purpose for writing and on an intended audience. Consider writing a short story, a fable or myth, a personal essay, a newspaper editorial, poetry, a dialogue, a short playscript, or a letter. In reality, you are limited only by the power of your imagination!

   a) I never knew so young a body with so old a head.

   b) So shines a good deed in a naughty world.

   c) O me, the word "choose"!

   d) He finds the joys of heaven here on earth.

   e) All things that are,
      Are with more spirit chased than enjoy'd.

   f) I have much ado to know myself.

   g) Alack, what heinous sin is it in me
      To be asham'd to be my father's child!

   h) O what a goodly outside falsehood hath!

   i) It is a wise father that knows his own child.

   j) The man that hath no music in himself . . .
      Let no such man be trusted.

   Be sure to "publish" your work, sharing it with other members of the class and contributing it to your school or community paper or magazine.

8. Stereotypes need not be religious, national, or cultural. We live each day surrounded by more common stereotypes: the misunderstood teenager, the right-wing bigot, the bleeding-heart liberal, the ineffectual parent, the befuddled teacher. These stereotypes abound on television and radio and in films, comic strips, and music videos.

   In a small group, collect as many examples of media stereotyping as you can. Sort and label your evidence in order to arrive at categories that classify the kinds of stereotyping you have found. Sort your evidence again according to the intentions and purposes the examples seem to serve. A third sorting might measure the degree of harm or danger you find in each example.

Report the group's conclusions to the class. Allow enough time for discussion and response.

9.   The Passover prayer book, the *Haggadah*, contains the following statement:

"In every generation, someone rises up against us, to annihilate us."

Starting with a good encyclopedia, survey the history of anti-Semitic persecution in Europe and North America. Select a single example and research it in detail. Focus on the political, historical, and economic causes and repercussions of the persecution rather than the accumulation of statistics and details. Share your discoveries and observations with your group, and prepare a presentation to the class. Allow time for full discussion and response.

You may choose instead to relate the character of Shylock to the history of anti-Semitic literature and stereotyping both before and after the play was written. How might the depiction of Shylock originally have been influenced by earlier depictions of Jews in literature and art, and how has it in turn influenced European and North American attitudes toward Jews in the last 400 years?

You might find the following books helpful:

Chazan, Robert: *Medieval Stereotypes and Modern Anti-Semitism*
Dimont, Max I.: *Jews, God and History*
Flannery, Edward H.: *The Anguish of the Jews*
Johnson, Paul: *A History of the Jews*
Potok, Chaim: *Wanderings: History of the Jews*
Roth, Cecil: *The History of Jews in Venice*

10. Read one of the following novels, biographies, or autobiographies of more recent times as a companion piece to *The Merchant of Venice*. In all of these works, the

issue of racial or cultural prejudice is important. Prepare a "book talk" for your group or class, in which you review the book and comment upon its similarities and parallels with *The Merchant of Venice*. Consider especially the causes and effects of prejudice in the book.

Biographies

Bennet, Levone: *What Manner of Man (Martin Luther King, Jr.)*
Broadfoot, Barry: *Years of Sorrow, Years of Shame*
Frank, Anne: *Diary of a Young Girl*
Griffin, John H.: *Black Like Me*
Kuper, Jack: *Child of the Holocaust*
Kwinta, Chava: *I'm Still Living*
Malcolm X and Alex Haley: *The Autobiography of Malcolm X*
Meir, Golda: *My Life*
Peterson, Oscar, with Richard Palmer: *A Jazz Odyssey: The Life of Oscar Peterson*
Suzuki, David: *Metamorphosis*

Fiction

Achebe, Chinua: *Things Fall Apart*
Ball, John: *In the Heat of the Night*
Bock, Richard: *The Ash Garden*
Bonham, Frank: *Chief*
Cameron, Anne: *Daughters of Copper Woman*
Campbell, Maria: *Half-breed*
Craven, Margaret: *I Heard the Owl Call My Name*
Gaines, Ernest J.: *A Lesson Before Dying*
Greene, Betty: *Summer of My German Soldier*
Greene, Hannah: *I Never Promised You a Rose Garden*
Gutterson, David: *Snow Falling on Cedars*
Haley, Alex: *Roots*
Hegi, Ursula: *Stones From the River*
Hinton, S.E.: *The Outsiders*
Keyes, Daniel: *Flowers for Algernon*
Kogawa, Joy: *Obasan*
Leavitt, David: *Family Dancing*
Lee, Harper: *To Kill a Mockingbird*
Malamud, Bernard: *The Fixer*
Markandaya, Kamale: *The Nowhere Man*
Marlyn, John: *Under the Ribs of Death*

Marshall, James Vance: *Walkabout*
Richter, Hans P.: *Friedrich*
Samuels, Gertrude: *Mottele*
Sedaris, David: *Me Talk Pretty One Day*
Steinbeck, John: *Of Mice and Men*
Such, Peter: *Riverrun*
Ten Boom, Corrie: *The Hiding Place*
Walker, Alice: *The Color Purple*
White, Edmund: *A Boy's Own Story*
Wiesel, Elie: *Night*
Wright, Richard: *Native Son*

Your teacher or librarian could discuss these and other books with you and assist you in making a selection.

11. Many schools and school boards have decided that *The Merchant of Venice* is an unsuitable play for classroom study, on the grounds that it may be offensive to some students.

   From your study of the play, list the reasons you think some people might be offended by it. What is your own response to each of these objections? Do you consider them sufficient grounds for removing the play from the curriculum? What aspects of the play make it important to examine in spite of the controversy that surrounds it?

   In a small group, discuss these issues fully, giving careful and thoughtful consideration to the point of view of every member of the group. Organize and record the conclusions you reach in a personal essay, position paper, or short speech.

12. Since the twentieth century, responses to *The Merchant of Venice* seem to suggest that modern society has become more concerned about the rights and freedoms of individuals and minority groups. Many events and movements have contributed to our growing understanding and tolerance of others:

   a) the suffragettes

   b) the Holocaust

   c) the creation of the United Nations

   d) the American civil rights movement

e) women's liberation

f) the defeat of apartheid in South Africa

g) Third World refugees

h) Amnesty International

i) the fight for gay rights

Investigate one of these (or another important example of which you are aware). Discover the causes, the issues, and the results or repercussions of the group or event you select. Concentrate on the ways it has changed our attitudes toward others.

Present your observations and conclusions in an essay or class report. Alternatively, create a docudrama (a fictionalized drama based on historical fact) using your research to illuminate the issue. Narrow your focus to a single representative event or person.

13. Shakespeare's comedies often contained a great deal of musical accompaniment as well as songs. In this play, there is one song, in Act 3, and an explicit reference to background music, in Act 5.

    Imagine you are the musical director of a new production of *The Merchant of Venice.* It is your job to decide what music to use and where to use it to enhance the dramatic effect of the play. Do some research on the kind of music Shakespeare would have expected, but do not feel bound to stick to the music of the Renaissance. Be prepared to defend your selections (or original compositions!) with a presentation to the class.

    You might also submit a CD containing your selections. If you do, include the cover art (found or created) that best reflects the music you have chosen. Remember that cover art should help to sell the music to a wide audience.

14. With a group, choose a scene of interest to you and prepare it for presentation to your classmates or to a wider audience, using a Director's Notebook to guide your efforts. For the Director's Notebook, your group should complete the following tasks:

    a) An introductory report, in which you answer the following questions:

- Which characters are in this scene?
- What are the main events of the scene?
- What is the main purpose of the scene?

b) A character analysis for each character, in which you answer the following questions:

  - In this scene, what does the character want?
  - What obstacles does the character meet?
  - What happens when the character meets these obstacles?
  - What is distinctive about this character's way of speaking, gestures, or the language that she or he uses?

c) A *promptsheet*, on which you record decisions about blocking and delivery of lines. A promptsheet is a version of the script with wide margins on which directors and stage managers write notes about movement and direction.

d) Costume designs for each of the characters. Create two versions of the design—one for use in a classroom production, and one that you would create if your budget were unlimited. Consider:

  - In which era will you set the scene?
  - What effect do you want the costumes to have on the audience?
  - What will the costumes reveal about the characters and theme?

  Include a short explanation with your designs explaining the rationale behind your choices.

e) A set design for the scene. Create two versions of the design—one for a classroom production, and one that you would create if your budget were unlimited. Consider:

  - In which era will you set the scene?
  - What effect do you want the set to have on the audience?
  - What will the set reveal about the characters and theme?

f) A soundtrack for the scene. Create a tape or CD that will accompany your presentation of the scene. Include with it:
- a copy of any lyrics associated with the music you have chosen
- a short explanation of why you have chosen each sound effect or piece of music
- a CD or tape cover that might help you market the soundtrack in stores

Be sure to create a cover page for your Director's Notebook that includes your acting company's name and identifies the scene you have chosen.

15. In Shakespeare's time, the role of women was much more tightly defined than it is now. It would have been unusual in his day for a woman—even one of the upper classes—to wield as much power as Portia does in the play. Furthermore, notions about women at that time would have made Portia's behaviour in the play quite incredible.

Research the role of women in Elizabethan England. What stereotypes existed about women's abilities? In what ways were women's roles restricted? How did the average woman's lifestyle differ from that of one particularly famous woman, Queen Elizabeth I? What conclusions can you draw about Shakespeare's portrayal of women in *The Merchant of Venice*? Was Shakespeare the first feminist?

Some sources that may help you are:

Emerson, Kathy Lynn: *Wives and Daughters: The Women of 16th Century England*
Mendelson, Sarah Hellen and Patricia Crawford: *Women in Early Modern England 1550–1800*
Prior, Margot and Mary Prior: *Women in English Society 1500–1800*

Present your findings as an oral report or a research essay.

16. At the time that Shakespeare wrote, Jews had been expelled from England. It is unlikely that he would ever, in fact, have met a Jew. This may be why his portrayal of Shylock draws on negative stereotypes about Jewish people.

Research the history of Jews during the Elizabethan era

in Europe. What were the customs and beliefs that guided them in day-to-day life? What challenges did they face? How did they overcome these obstacles? Two books that may help you are *A History of the Jews* by Paul Johnson and *Jews, God and History* by Max I. Dimont. You may find other sources by searching the Internet or your library.

Create a report in the form of a magazine article to inform the people of Shakespeare's time about the reality of being Jewish in sixteenth-century Europe.

17. The "casket" subplot is reminiscent of television game shows such as "The Price Is Right." Using the characters involved in this plot, create an episode of a new game show in which Portia is the host and her suitors are the contestants. Capture this "episode" of the show on video or perform it live for your class.

18. Choose two of the main characters in *The Merchant of Venice* and create a *character map* for each.

    To create a character map, place the character's name in the centre of the map. At the next level, choose four traits that describe the character. At the third level, find three pieces of evidence for each trait.

    For example:

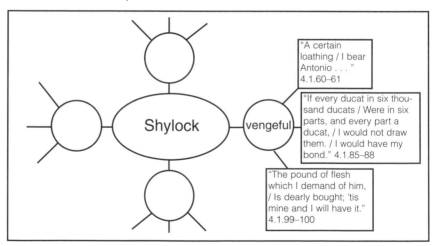

Using the character map, write an essay in which you compare and contrast the characters' traits. What conclusions can you draw as a result? Include these in the final paragraph of your essay.